OLIVER CROMWELL

PROFILES IN POWER

General Editor: Keith Robbins

. . . .

OLIVER CROMWELL

Barry Coward

LONGMAN
London and New York

Longman Group UK Limited
Longman House, Burnt Mill, Harlow
Essex CM20 2JE, England
and Associated Companies throughout the world.

*Published in the United States of America
by Longman Inc.. New York*

First published 1991
Second impression 1992

British Library Cataloguing in Publication Data
A catalogue record for this book is available from the British Library

ISBN 0-582-08725-2
ISBN 0-582-55385-7 pbk

Library of Congress Cataloging in Publication Data
Coward, Barry
Oliver Cromwell/Barry Coward.
p. cm. — (Profiles in power)
Includes bibliographical references and index.
ISBN 0-582-08725-2 (csd)
ISBN 0-582-55385-7 (ppr)
1. Cromwell, Oliver, 1599–1658. 2. Generals—Great Britain—
Biography. 3. Heads of state—Great Britain—Biography.
4. Great Britain—History—Puritan Revolution, 1642–1660. I. Title.
II. Series: Profiles in power (London, England)
DA426.C68 1991
941.06'4'092—dc20
[B]   91—2405
                                        CIP

Set in Baskerville

Produced by Longman Singapore Publishers (Pte) Ltd.
Printed in Singapore

CONTENTS

· · · · · ·

ABBREVIATIONS AND ACKNOWLEDGEMENTS

In the Notes and References at the end of each chapter the following abbreviations are used:

Abbott: W.C. Abbott (ed.), *The Writings and Speeches of Oliver Cromwell* (4 vols, Cambridge. Mass., 1937–47)

Original Letters: J. Nickolls (ed.), *Original Letters and Papers of State Addressed to Oliver Cromwell . . . etc.* (1843)

TSP : Thomas Birch (ed.), *A Collection of the State Papers of John Thurloe.* (7 vols, 1742)

Of the many people who have helped me, wittingly and unwittingly, in writing this book, I would like to thank particularly Professor Anthony Fletcher, of the University of Durham, who read and made valuable comments on a draft of the first seven chapters.

. . . .

INTRODUCTION

'Is another study of Oliver Cromwell needed?' has been a question I have been asked by some who have learned that I was writing this book. In one sense this is not a surprising question, as countless biographies of Cromwell exist. There are, however, two answers. The first is that this book is not a biography. Following the editorial guidelines of the series of which it is a part, it is a study of Cromwell as a political figure and of the historical problems associated with his exercise of power. Furthermore, many of these historical problems have never been satisfactorily answered. I make no claim that this book provides definitive answers to them. Indeed there have been times during its composition when my puzzlement about the man has increased, along with the conviction that the search for 'truths' about so complex and controversial a character as Oliver Cromwell is fraught with more obstacles than historians usually face in the normal course of their work. In these circumstances my aim is merely to suggest answers to some of the problems raised by Cromwell's political career.

These problems are, of course, legion. What conclusions about Cromwell's political ·aims and ambitions can be drawn from the handful of evidence that survives about the first forty-one years of his life? How important a member of the parliamentary opposition to Charles I was he in the packed, fast-moving months between the calling of the Long Parliament in November 1640 and the outbreak of the Civil War in August 1642? What drove him to brush aside the risks of being charged with treason by seizing money and plate bound from Cambridge to the king in August 1642 before the Civil War had officially begun?

Given Cromwell's lack of any previous military experience, how was it that he gained an extraordinarily high reputation as a cavalry commander in the Civil War? How well-deserved is that reputation? What was his part in the politicisation of the victorious parliamentary New Model Army after the war? Did he (as has sometimes been alleged) initiate the successful attempt by Cornet Joyce in June 1647 to capture the king from his parliamentary guards at Holmby House, which propelled the army into adopting a new political role? How seriously did Cromwell and others pursue negotiations with the king in 1647? What were Cromwell's aims at the famous Putney Debates in the army council at the end of the year, and did he engineer the king's escape from army custody in November 1647 in order to stifle the growing radical influence of the Levellers in the army ranks? What pushed Cromwell in the last days of 1648 to ditch any hopes he had of achieving a settlement with Charles I and to become one of the most fervent advocates of bringing the king to trial and execution?

His career after the establishment of the English Republic in 1649 is littered with (if anything) even more intractable problems that centre around explaining Cromwell's apparent 'ideological schizophrenia':[1] his phases of cautious moderation that were interrupted by explosive and outrageous outbursts of radical political activism. Why, after his return to parliament after crushing opposition to the new republic in Ireland and Scotland between 1649 and 1651, did he suddenly abandon months of hard work attempting to prevent the growth of renewed division between MPs and the army and, on 20 April 1653, backed by military force, angrily dissolve parliament? What were his intentions in then calling a nominated assembly, the so-called Barebones Parliament? Did he intend it to be a permanent rule of godly 'saints'? Why did he acquiesce in the political plot that brought about the end of Barebones Parliament and why did he agree to being installed as Protector of the Commonwealth of England, Ireland and Scotland in December 1653? How seriously did he work for a return to 'normal' modes of government by a single person and parliaments? Why did the two parliaments he called during his Protectorate both end with sudden outbursts of Cromwellian anger and frustration? What caused him to agree to the appointment of major-generals to exercise power in English provinces in the middle years of his Protectorate? Why did he accept a new parliamentary constitution and yet turn down the offer to become King Oliver I in 1657? Was his Protectorate a military dictatorship led by a man driven by vaulting ambition? As will be seen, the Cromwellian Protectorate was not simply a military dictatorship, and there is little doubt that Cromwell was driven throughout his career from the early 1640s by a growing and overwhelming desire to achieve much more than personal gain. What exactly he wanted to do with the power he held is, however, the most difficult, unresolved question of them all.

My second justification for producing yet another book on Cromwell is that so radically have historical interpretations of seventeenth-century British history changed in recent years that one cannot fail to be helped to find new approaches to many of these problems about Oliver Cromwell. The recent 'revisionist' wave on the causes of the Civil War has not produced anything like a consensus,[2] but the reasons for the growth of mistrust some felt at Charles I's government by 1640 are clearer now than they once were. It is possible to appreciate more fully the role of the fear of popery in shaping political attitudes. Important recent work on the nature of post-Reformation Protestantism and the national Church has clarified the place of the 'godly' – 'puritan' – minority in English society in the first half of the seventeenth century. Furthermore, the strength of social and political conservatism in England during the 'revolutionary' mid-century decades has been emphasised, as has the important role of the House of Lords and of the peerage in politics.

In tackling the many historical problems posed by Cromwell's political career in the context of this and other recent works on seventeenth-century Britain, many aspects have become clearer to me than when I first started work on this book, and have influenced what I have written. Of these, three stand out. The first is that Cromwell was not as dominant a figure in the politics of the 1640s and 1650s as I had previously assumed he was. In what follows he inevitably often takes the centre stage, but I have tried throughout not to exaggerate his importance unduly. Certainly before 1642 he was a very minor political figure, who, had it not been for his later exploits on the battlefield, would have deserved little more than a footnote in the historical accounts of that period. Even after the outbreak of the Civil War his importance was less than that of many others in the tangled politics of wartime and postwar England. Even at the climax of the English Revolution in the winter months of 1648–49 his role was not always a leading one. Moreover, as Protector he often ruled in England and in foreign affairs with the advice (as he was bound to do under the protectoral constitution, the Instrument of Government) of his council of state; and he left the day-to-day management of and direction of policy in conquered Ireland and Scotland largely to others.

The second thing that became apparent is that much the best way of understanding Cromwell's aims and activities is by adopting a chronological approach. S.R. Gardiner, writing in the preface to his four-volume *History of the Great Civil War* in the 1890s about some of the 'knotty matters' relating to Cromwell's political career, concluded that 'the thread leading out of the maze is to be found by a strict adherence to chronology. It is with no little surprise that I found one charge after another [made against Cromwell] melt away as I was able to fix a date to the words or actions which had given rise to hostile comment.'[3] Although not all (by any means) of the problems about Cromwell have melted away for me, much of what he did has become more explicable when discussed in their proper historical context. This accounts for my decision to give the book a chronological structure.

The third aspect has surprised me most of all. I had always thought that the main characteristic of Oliver Cromwell's political career was its inconsistency. There is no doubt that, as will be seen, Cromwell attempted to achieve aims that were, at the very least, difficult to reconcile, and that he was forced at times to choose between them. His career consequently does oscillate from moments of cautious temporising to bursts of radical action when he seems to have thrown caution to the winds. Yet, from a point in the early 1640s onwards, it will be argued, there is a *consistent* thread running through his career: the aims he de-

4

veloped during and immediately after the Civil War in debates on military campaigns and with political allies at Westminster remained the bedrock of his ambitions until the end of his life.

It is impossible to be certain exactly when these aims became fully formed. Before 1642, as will be seen in the first chapter, Cromwell was a shadowy and obscure figure, with little hint of the prominence he was to begin to gain within a few months of the outbreak of the Civil War.

· · ·

NOTES AND REFERENCES

1. B. Worden, *The Rump Parliament* (Oxford University Press, 1974), p. 69.
2. See the Bibliographical Essay.
3. S.R. Gardiner, *History of the Great Civil War 1642–49* (first published in 1893, reprint edn, Windrush Press, 1987, 4 vols), vol. I, p. x.

Chapter 1

THE UNKNOWN CROMWELL
(1599–1642)

When the English Civil War began in August 1642 Oliver
Cromwell was forty-three years old, a man on the brink of
middle age. Before that date historians know as little about
him as did many of his contemporaries, for the simple reason that little source material on the 'prehistoric' Cromwell
before 1642 has survived. However, this has not stopped
people from inventing stories about him. 'Legends always
grow around the towering figures of history', wrote H.N.
Brailsford,[1] and Cromwell is no exception. A priority,
therefore, for anyone attempting to discover what kind of
man Cromwell was in 1642, before his rise began from obscurity to Lord Protector of England, Scotland and Ireland,
is to strip away layers of myths and legends about him,
rather as an archaeologist seeking evidence of earlier peo-
ples removes debris left by later civilisations. When that is
done, what is left, as will be seen, is merely a tiny handful
of disconnected 'facts' – the equivalent of the archaeologist's pieces of broken pottery and other artefacts – from
which to try to construct answers to the major questions
that are vital to an understanding of Cromwell's meteoric
rise to power and greatness in the last sixteen years of his
life. What kind of social and economic background did
Cromwell come from? How wealthy and socially influential
was he by the early 1640s? What were his religious and political views? How important was his role in the development of the powerful parliamentary opposition faced by
Charles I in the period before the outbreak of the Civil
War? What drove him to become in 1642 one of those
whom Sir Simonds D'Ewes called the 'fiery spirits', who,
brushing aside the risks he ran of losing his life and his

6

property, unhesitatingly committed himself to fighting against the king, even before the official outbreak of hostilities on 22 August 1642?

The sources of many of the apocryphal stories of Cromwell before 1642 are hostile biographies, written just after the Restoration, which gleefully printed invented, scandalous stories about him in order to blacken his character and portray him as a life-long enemy of the monarchy. Typical of these is the tale of Cromwell and Prince Charles meeting as toddlers when James I and his court stayed at the house of Cromwell's uncle, Sir Oliver Cromwell, at Hinchingbrook in the early 1600s, and Cromwell was said to have bloodied the young prince's nose. James Heath, Cromwell's most imaginative early biographer in his book, *Flagellum, or the Life and Death, Birth and Burial of Oliver Cromwell, the Late Usurper*, had no compunction in retailing invented stories of Cromwell's youth. During his short stay as a student at Cambridge University Heath alleged that Cromwell 'was more famous for his exercises in the Field than in the Schools (in which he never had the honour of, because no worth and merit to, a degree) being one of the chief match-makers and players at Foot-ball, Cudgels, or any other boysterous sport or game'.[2] After he left Cambridge, Heath described Cromwell neglecting his legal studies at one of the capital's Inns of Court for 'uncontrolled debaucheries . . . Drinking, Wenching, and the like outrages of licentious youth'.[3] Heath's diatribes are very quotable, but must be disregarded as malicious inventions that tell one far more about the overwhelming tide of hatred for Cromwell felt by many influential people in Restoration England (witnessed, for example, in the exhumation and 'execution' of Cromwell's body in 1661) than they do about Cromwell's early life. Equally interesting, but nevertheless of little value for an understanding of Cromwell's career, are the folk-legends that have grown round Cromwell's name. One example of this is the persistent myth of Cromwell the destroyer of churches, which seems to have originated in a confusion of Oliver with Thomas Cromwell, Henry VIII's agent in carrying out the dissolution of church property about sixty years before Oliver was born.

Other stories that have become attached to Cromwell

cannot be treated quite so dismissively. In this category are the tantalising legends that Cromwell travelled on the Continent at some time in the 1620s or 1630s, not only meeting on his travels the Jewish leader, Menasseh ben Israel, with whom Cromwell corresponded later as Protector, but also serving as a soldier in a European army during the Thirty Years' War. These (if true) would help to explain the difficult puzzles of Cromwell's later conversion to the cause of the readmission of the Jews to England, as well as his remarkable success as a soldier in the Civil War and on later military campaigns in Ireland and Scotland. But for these stories – as well as for the legend that Cromwell in the 1630s once boarded a ship intending to emigrate to New England, but disembarked before it set sail – there exists no supporting evidence at all. There is some reason to accept later stories that Cromwell spent some time at one of the Inns of Court getting a smattering of legal knowledge, since it was not unusual for youths from Cromwell's background to complete their education in this way. But it is by no means certain that he did so. There is no record of his name in any admissions register of an Inn of Court, and Cromwell himself later disclaimed any great knowledge of legal technicalities: 'I have heard talk of "demurrers" and such like things as I scarce know of', he told a Commons committee on 21 April 1657.[4]

Recently, too, other episodes that are well-entrenched as part of the Cromwell legend have been shown to have been misunderstood and will no longer bear the significance they once had. Perhaps the most surprising recent suggestion, made by John Morrill, is that it is highly unlikely either that Cromwell's religious views were decisively shaped (as has long been assumed) by his Huntingdon schoolmaster, Dr Thomas Beard and by Beard's book, *A Theatre of Judgement*, or that Beard was a Puritan role-model for his young pupil. Beard was 'a greedy pluralist', schoolmaster, vicar of All Saints parish in Huntingdon, warden of the hospital there and also vicar of Kimbolton. He later surrendered the latter office after becoming vicar of St John's parish in Huntingdon in 1610. Morrill, with much patient detective work, has revealed that Beard in 1630 greedily tried to get his hand on a further source of income, a bequest given to the burgesses of Huntingdon by the London Mercers' Company to establish a new preaching lectureship in the town, which supports his case that Beard 'looks like a complacent Jacobean Calvinist conformist: not the man to ignite the fire in Cromwell's belly'.[5] Nor should much of later significance be read into the fragmentary evidence relating to Cromwell's election to the parliament of 1628–29 as MP for Huntingdon. The incomplete versions of Cromwell's only speech in that parliament, in which he seems merely to have described an incident that had happened at least ten years before in order to illustrate the fear he shared with other MPs of the spread of Arminianism among the episcopacy, suggest that he played a very minor part in the parliament that produced the Petition of Right. The evidence simply does not exist to support the notion that Cromwell's first parliamentary experience presaged his later important role in parliamentary politics from the mid–1640s onwards. Moreover, when one looks closely at the legend of Cromwell's political 'opposition' to the monarchy and established authority in the 1630s, the sources for it all but disappear. Brian Quintrell has shown that no evidence exists to suggest that Cromwell stood as a principled opponent of distraint of knighthood, one of Charles I's new, unpopular financial levies during his Personal Rule after the dissolution of parliament in 1629.[6] Moreover, the legend of Cromwell as 'Lord of the Fens', an opponent of the capitalist syndicates of merchants and aristocratic courtiers who in the 1630s were attempting to drain and enclose large tracts of fenland in and around Ely, is based mainly on one fragmentary report in 1638 that the inhabitants of the Ely fens had made an agreement with Cromwell: 'they paying him a groat for every cow they had upon the common, to hold the drainers in suit for five years and in the meantime they should enjoy every foot of their common'.[7] Even if this were true, it is not proof that Cromwell was against fen drainage. In fact he later supported it as Protector. Rather he was probably concerned to ensure that those dispossessed by the drainage schemes should be compensated. There are no real grounds for believing that Cromwell was a radical champion of popular rights or a leading opponent of Charles I's fiscal expedients in the 1630s.

When these and other myths and legends are discounted

one is left with a very sketchy *curriculum vitae* of the man who was elected as MP for Cambridge to the Short and Long Parliaments in the two elections of 1640. He was born on 25 April 1599 in Huntingdon, near Cambridge, in eastern England, the only surviving son of Robert and Elizabeth Cromwell, who also had seven daughters (Cromwell's elder sisters, Joan, Elizabeth and Catherine, and his younger sisters, Margaret, Anna, Jane and Robina). He was educated at the local Huntingdon Free Grammar School, where Thomas Beard was schoolmaster, and then for just over a year at Sidney Sussex College, Cambridge University, from April 1616 to June 1617. His university studies were cut short by his father's death and he left Cambridge to take over the running of his father's property in and around Huntingdon. In 1620 he married Elizabeth Bouchier, the daughter of a wealthy London fur-dealer and leather dresser, whom he may have met in London or in Essex where the Bouchiers had some property, including Little Stanbrook Hall near Felsted in Essex. All the evidence, including the births of eight children between 1621 and 1638 points to the fact that theirs was a close, warm relationship and no-one has found any evidence to substantiate later Royalist allegations about Cromwell's marital infidelities.[8]

The only other major events in the lives of the Cromwell family before 1640 about which one can be certain is that they moved home twice: once in 1631 when Cromwell sold most of his property in Huntingdon and moved to St Ives, five miles away; and then again in 1636 when the family moved to Ely. Only twice are there undisputed records of Cromwell moving out of East Anglia before 1640, once when he went to London as MP for Huntingdon in the parliament of 1628–29, and again in 1630 when he appeared before the privy council concerning a local dispute over the Huntingdon town charter.

Cromwell later said (in a speech to parliament in 1654) that he was 'by birth a gentleman living neither in considerable height nor yet in obscurity'.[9] How accurate is that as an indication of what is now known of his economic and social standing before 1640? There is no doubt that Cromwell was 'by birth a gentleman'. His grandfather and uncle, Sir Henry and Sir Oliver Cromwell, held substantial property in Huntingdonshire and elsewhere, including a great house at Hinchingbrook, just outside Huntingdon, and their lifestyles were appropriate to their positions as county magnates, serving as JPs and MPs. Cromwell had sound family connections: two of his aunts, for example, married into prominent gentry families, the Hampdens of Buckinghamshire and the Barringtons of Essex, and a cousin married Oliver St John. These also placed him, for most of his life before 1640, just above the greatest gulf in early modern English society: that separating gentlemen from the rest. The little that is known of Cromwell's educational career is typical of that followed by sons of early seventeenth-century gentlemen, especially if Cromwell did study at an Inn of Court as well as at Cambridge University. Moreover, Cromwell's marriage to the daughter of a wealthy and well-connected London merchant and Essex landowner consolidated his claims to gentility, which were also reflected in his election to parliament in 1628. However, Cromwell before 1640 was always on the fringes of East Anglian gentry society, and for a short time in the early 1630s he may have fallen into the ranks of the yeomanry, a reminder of the fact that the gulf between gentry and non-gentry was bridgeable downwards as well as upwards in the early seventeenth century. Cromwell's status cannot fail to have been adversely affected by the fact that his uncle's economic position declined sharply in the 1620s, signified by the sale of Hinchingbrook to the Montagues, who replaced the senior Cromwells as the leading patriarchs of the region. More importantly, his father's inheritance, as a younger son in a society in which primogeniture was dominant among the propertied classes, was fairly small. When it was sold in 1631 for £1,800 it was probably worth only £90 a year (assuming the normal formula of assessing land prices was used, i.e. twenty times its annual gross value), making Cromwell only a very minor gentleman indeed when he inherited the property in 1617. What is more, fourteen years later, his economic situation took a sharp turn for the worse. His decision to move to St Ives in 1631 may have been occasioned by the backwash of a political controversy in which Cromwell became involved in Huntingdon, but the move was one of a family clearly sliding down the social scale. Cromwell sold all his property in Huntingdon (except seventeen acres) and became the tenant of a small farm in St Ives, adopting the lifestyle of a yeoman farmer rather than a landowning gentleman. In 1636 his economic fortunes were salvaged, when he became the major legatee of his mother's brother's will, inheriting tithes and glebe land in Ely and the house on the edge of the cathedral green in which his mother had been born (his mother and unmarried sisters joined him and his family there) with an income of about £300 a year. Though the evidence is sparse, it suggests that by the later 1630s Cromwell had clawed his way back into the ranks of the gentry – just.

There is, if anything, even less evidence on which to build a picture of Cromwell's attitudes to politics before 1640. As has been seen, it is now no longer possible to portray Cromwell as a leading political activist against the policies of Charles I throughout the later 1620s and 1630s. In the 1630s Cromwell paid his ship money dues, as well as the fine for distraint of knighthood levied by the Crown. Nor does the quarrel he had in Huntingdon in 1630 with those who secured a new charter for the town seem to have been one in which Cromwell displayed principled opposition to oligarchic rule. Cromwell's main complaint against the new charter when the case was heard before the privy council was that the new rulers of the town might use their influence to promote their own selfish purposes and, perhaps equally important, that he had not been appointed alderman under the new arrangements.

Why, then, was Cromwell a determined opponent of the king from the start of the first session of the Long Parliament in November 1640? One answer to this question is that Cromwell was politicised by his religious views. At some time before 1638 Cromwell was converted to a set of religious values that made him increasingly concerned at the religious policies pursued by Charles I. During his late twenties or early thirties he underwent a spiritual experience that convinced him that God had appointed him to be one of the Elect, chosen for eternal salvation. In one of his fullest early letters, written on 13 October 1638 to his cousin's wife, Mrs St John, he describes his conversion in graphic terms:

God . . . giveth springs in a dry and barren wilderness
where no water is. I live (you know where) in Mesheck,
which they say signifies Prolonging; in Kedar, which signifies Blackness: yet the Lord forsaketh me not. Though
He do prolong, yet He will (I trust) bring me to His
tabernacle, to His resting-place. My soul is with the congregation of the firstborn, my body rests in hope, and if
here I may honour my God either by doing or by suffer-
ing, I shall be most glad . . . the Lord accepts me in
His Son, and give me to walk in the light, as He is in the
light . . . . Blessed be His name for shining upon so
dark a heart as mine! You know what my manner of life
hath been. Oh, have I lived in and loved darkness, and
hated the light. I was a chief, the chief of sinners. This is
true; I hated godliness, yet God had mercy on me. O the
riches of His mercy![10]

It is impossible to be certain when this conversion occurred. It may not have happened suddenly, as is often assumed. What is probable is that it was completed by about
1629 or 1630, following an attack of ill-health. As will be
seen Cromwell often suffered from illnesses at times of
spiritual and political crises. When he was in London for
the parliamentary session of 1628–29 he consulted Dr The-
odore Mayerne, a well-known London physician, who reported in his casebook that Cromwell suffered from
depression ('*valde melancholicus*'). At some time, too, he was
visited by his own doctor, Dr Simcotts of Huntingdon, who
later told Sir Philip Warwick that 'he had been called up to
him very many times upon a strong fancy, which made him
believe he was dying'.[11] It may be that these bouts of depression and hypochondria presaged the completion of his
spiritual conversion. However, there is a danger of seeing
all Cromwell's illnesses as being symptoms of crises in his
public and private life. Clearly this was not the case; in
1645 a journalist who knew him well, John Dillingham, reported that Cromwell was sick because he had 'surfeited of
green Plumbs'.[12] What is even more likely than its specific
date or cause (for which there is little direct evidence) is
that his spiritual experience was one shared by other later
sixteenth- and early seventeenth-century 'godly' Protestants, about whom much is now known.[13] It is not stretch-

ing the evidence too far (and it certainly fits in with what is known of Cromwell's religious beliefs after 1642) to suggest that Cromwell after his conversion came to share the life-style and beliefs of the 'godly' minority of early Stuart England.

The prime characteristic of the 'godly' was a commitment to further (or complete) the Reformation. Like other 'godly' men and women in this period, Cromwell came to believe that the Reformation of the mid-sixteenth century was a misnomer; it was at best a half-Reformation. Although the Reformation had destroyed the authority of the Pope in the English Church, pre-Reformation officials, including bishops, survived and Catholic rituals, such as the wearing of vestments by clergy and Catholic festivals such as Christmas, were still allowed. And, worst of all, not only had there been only a partial Reformation of Church government and liturgy, a spiritual inner reformation of the people of England had made even less progress. Sinfulness, drunkenness, swearing, fornication, adultery and bastardy abounded, despite a long 'godly' campaign from at least the 1580s to counter them. At his 'conversion', therefore, Cromwell became part of a determined campaign (though mounted by a minority in England) to complete the Reformation in Church government and liturgy, and to bring about a 'godly' inner reformation of people's lives as well.

Before 1640, however, the campaign did not include an attack on the structure of Church government or on the notion of one national Church. The main thrust of the campaign to advance a godly reformation was to create the conditions within the national Church to allow individuals to find God for themselves freely, as long as they did not disturb the peace or attack the existing social and political order. Indeed, the main leaders of the campaign for godly reformation in the 1630s were pillars of the existing social and political order, a circle of peers led by the earls of Bedford and Warwick and Lord Saye and Sele, who were closely associated with non-aristocratic, wealthy gentlemen such as John Pym, John Hampden and Oliver St John. In explaining the transformation by 1640 of men like these with conservative political views into keen opponents of the monarchy, the importance of Charles I's attempt to promote Arminianism in the English Church cannot be exaggerated. Arminianism not only represented an attack on the prevailing Calvinist predestinarian theology, held by the majority of English Protestants, in favour of the theology of free will, but its proponents (principally William Laud, Archbishop of Canterbury from 1633) whom Charles I promoted to positions of power in the English Church also favoured a type of church service that appeared to many Protestants to be as near to Catholicism as to make no difference. They attempted to impose this liturgy on English parishes, displacing in some cases forms of worship that had been practised since the later sixteenth century. Laud's attempts to promote the sacramental and ceremonial aspects of church services at the expense of sermons were especially regarded by some as an attempt to undo, not further, the Reformation. Moreover, the fact that Charles I allowed his wife, Henrietta Maria, and foreign ambassadors in London to hold Catholic masses, and that the king himself received papal agents at court, gave credence to a growing suspicion held by some that Protestantism was endangered by an organised Popish Plot centred on the court.

What also added force to escalating suspicions of the court among the godly was the fear that some people round the king (if not Charles I himself) were mounting an attack not only on Protestantism but also on the existing constitution. It is now possible to see the pressures that forced Charles I and his ministers, having entered a major war against France and Spain in the mid-1620s, to seek extra-parliamentary sources of income, such as forced loans. Traditional means of raising money used hitherto by the English monarchy were not adequate to fight major continental wars. But Charles, not only attempted to raise money in the 1620s by extraordinary means, he also imprisoned men who refused to submit to his demands. Moreover, in the 1630s, even though the country was now at peace, he continued to attempt to raise money by expedients such as ship money when parliament was not in session. In these conditions it is highly likely that by the end of the decade the fears of godly Protestants for the survival of Protestantism and of parliament were indistinguishable. Their aims of a godly reformation, they believed, could be achieved only if Charles I returned to traditional

15

ways of government, ruling with the advice of his greater magnates and with regular parliaments.

There is little doubt that Cromwell shared these views in 1640, since many of his activities in the early months of the Long Parliament were directed towards the cause of furthering the Reformation. Among the many committees to which he was appointed were the important grand committee of religion and committees to consider complaints against the Laudian bishop of Ely and the introduction of a parliamentary bill 'for the abolition of superstition and idolatry and for the better advancement of the true worship and service of God'.[14] It was Cromwell's motion on 8 September 1641 that led to a Commons' vote that 'sermons should be in the afternoons in all parishes of England'.[15] Moreover, before the outbreak of the Civil War his name frequently recurs in the parliamentary campaign against bishops and the Book of Common Prayer. Sir Edward Dering (later regretting what he had done) said that the draft bill he introduced into the Commons on 29 May to abolish the hierarchy of the English Church, including archbishops and bishops, was 'pressed into my hand' by Sir Arthur Haselrig, who had been given it by Henry Vane junior and Oliver Cromwell.[16]

Cromwell may also have been on the outer fringes of the political clique that led the opposition to the king in 1640. Much has been made in the past of Cromwell's family relationships with many parliamentary critics of the king in the early 1640s. As has been seen, he had connections by blood and marriage with John Hampden and Oliver St John. His aunt's marriage into the Barrington family brought him into contact with the powerful clientage of the earl of Warwick in the county of Essex. Moreover, four of Cromwell's sons went to Felsted school in Essex, whose headmaster was appointed by Warwick. It has recently been suggested that such links with some of the most powerful men in eastern England are a plausible explanation for Cromwell's election in 1640 as MP for Cambridge to sit in both the Short and Long Parliaments.[17] Yet it must be emphasised that evidence that Cromwell was *closely* allied to the parliamentary leadership at this stage does not exist. Even after the start of the Long Parliament in November 1640 (when evidence of Cromwell's activities becomes more abundant) it is difficult to be certain how closely Cromwell worked with peers like Bedford, Warwick, Saye and Sele in the House of Lords and their allies in the Commons, led by John Pym. The fact that Cromwell occasionally played a more prominent role in proceedings in the Commons than one would expect of someone of his political inexperience suggests that his family connections and religious and political views at least pulled him into the orbit of these great men at Westminster. It is difficult otherwise to explain why it was Cromwell who, only six days after the start of the Long Parliament, presented the petition of one of the parliamentary heroes of the early days of the Long Parliament, John Lilburne, against sentence passed on him by the Star Chamber. Much of what he did in 1640–41 is consistent with the view that he was entrusted by the parliamentary leaders in both houses of parliament with carrying out some of their political initiatives. On 30 December 1640 Cromwell moved the second reading of a bill for annual parliaments, which a few months later became the Triennial Act; in August 1641 he proposed that Saye and Sele and Bedford be made guardians of the Prince of Wales; and in the autumn of 1641 he suggested that the earl of Essex be appointed commander of the militia by parliamentary ordinance, not by a parliamentary bill that would require the king's assent.

However, all this is not enough evidence to suggest that Cromwell was yet a figure of *central* importance among the king's opponents. For one thing it is dangerous to assume at any time that family relationships are necessarily the basis for firm political alliances. Common sense suggests that love and affection is by no means the only type of relationship that exists between members of extended families. What above all sounds a warning note against describing Cromwell as a figure of major consequence in the politics of the early months of the Long Parliament is that he made too many political gaffes to gain the confidence of the parliamentary leadership. Impulsive behaviour is a consistent feature of Cromwell's career, as will be seen. But in the early days of his parliamentary career his excitability and impetuosity made him a political liability. Already it had got him into trouble during the row over the Huntingdon charter in 1630, when he was reprimanded by the privy council for making 'disgraceful and unseemly speeches' against the mayor of the town.[18] On many occasions before the outbreak of the Civil War his interventions in the Commons were ill-considered, naive and counterproductive, and must have been viewed with alarm by the parliamentary leaders. On one occasion, in February 1641, his anxiety to defend those (like himself) who attacked bishops against the charge of Sir John Strangeways that 'if wee made a paritie in the church wee must at last come to a paritie in the Commonwealth' led him to denounce Strangeways in a violent speech for which he was reprimanded by the House.[19] A few months later (though the source, Sir Edward Hyde, later one of Charles I's main supporters, is not objective) Cromwell was said to have acted with 'much indecency and rudeness' and to have spoken 'in language so contrary and offensive' to Lord Mandeville (later earl of Manchester) when the question of fen drainage came before a Commons' committee.[20] Moreover, some of Cromwell's interventions in parliamentary affairs at the time were at best naive and were recognised as such at the time. His proposal in February 1642 that his fellow MP, John Moore, should be asked to write a refutation of a collection of speeches by Sir Edward Dering, who was now attempting to distance himself from his earlier attacks on bishops, may only have caused irritation to Moore, who clearly had not been consulted beforehand by Cromwell. But Cromwell's naivety was clear for all to see in October 1641 when he argued that the proposal that bishops should not vote in parliament on a bill to exclude them permanently from the House of Lords was only a temporary measure until the bill was passed. 'The gentleman it seemes', wrote Sir Simonds D'Ewes scornfully in his diary, 'did not consider that if wee could but suspend their [the bishops'] voices for a time till the Bill wee have sent upp were past they must for ever loose their Votes in the Lords howse'.[21]

Incidents such as these are a clue to what are much more important features of Cromwell's career at this stage than the minor place he had among the king's parliamentary opponents before the Civil War. His impetuosity and naivety demonstrate his confidence in the rightness of what he was doing, his unquestioning conviction that the cause of parliament and that of godly reformation were indistinguishable, and his growing fear that unless measures were not taken soon the cause would be lost. This led him to fail to see the need for political guile. It also caused him to make political miscalculations, such as his forecast that few would oppose the Grand Remonstrance, a long document, spelling out the parliamentary case against the king. In fact, many conservative-minded MPs voted against the Grand Remonstrance and it was passed on 22 November 1641 by only a narrow majority of eleven votes. They voiced their fears at the radical drift of events, but Cromwell apparently shared none of their qualms. Indeed, on the contrary, the events of 1640–41 strengthened his determination to defend parliament. When the details of a series of plots among the English army in northern England were revealed by the parliamentary leaders in 1641, Cromwell was among those who pressed for the prosecution of those implicated in the plots, opposing their release on bail. It is not surprising, therefore, that when the king decided to go to Scotland in August 1641 Cromwell was among those who opposed the visit, fearing that Charles, would conspire with northern enemies of the parliamentary cause (as in fact proved to be the case). Above all, what caused Cromwell, again like many others, most alarm was the news of the Irish Rebellion, which reached London on 1 November 1641. Eight years later the horror of what he called 'the most unheard-of and most barbrous massacre (without respect of sex or age) that ever the sun beheld' was undiminished.[22] Like other Protestant Englishmen, he saw the Irish Rebellion not as an uprising against the harshness and oppression of English rule in seventeenth-century Ireland, but as an outrage committed by Catholics as the first step to an invasion of England, the reversal of the Reformation and the return of England to Catholicism. He was desperate to counter the threat. At the end of 1641 he pressed for command of the army in Ireland to be given to Owen O'Connell who had been instrumental in revealing details of the rising when it first began; early in 1642 he reported to the Commons 'dangerous words' spoken in London by an Irish Catholic;[23] and in April 1642 he sat on the newly appointed Council for Irish Affairs. Between April and July 1642 he invested £2,050 in the expedition planned by the 'adventurers' established by act of parliament in March 1642 for the reconquest of Ireland. What may also have intensified his anxiety was his correspondence and contacts with 'godly' people in the provinces who shared his unease. Early in 1642 Richard Symmonds of Abergavenny, a Puritan minister and schoolmaster client of Sir Robert Harley, sent Cromwell, Pym and Heselrige a petition, which Cromwell presented to the Commons, that 'if some speedy cause were not taken [to counter the strength of popery in Monmouthshire] it would be as great danger shortly as Ireland'.[24] Moreover, in July 1642 Sir William Brereton, who was to be one of the most determined leaders of the parliamentary war effort in north-west England, wrote to Cromwell, warning him of the severity being shown to Puritan ministers in Cheshire by Charles I's commissioners of array.

The overriding impression of Cromwell at this time is of a backbench MP driven by fear, which grew day by day as alarming news accumulated that, unless drastic measures were taken soon, then 'the cause' of parliamentary liberties and godly reformation would be destroyed. Very soon after the king's attempted counter-coup of 4 January 1642, in which he failed to arrest John Pym, Arthur Haselrig, Denzil Holles, William Strode, John Hampden and Lord Mandeville (whom he considered were leading the opposition to him), Cromwell joined those pressing for drastic measures. Ten days later he moved that a parliamentary committee be named to consider taking military measures against the threat he feared from Catholics and their sympathisers. He was not appointed a member of the so-called Militia Committee that was given this task, but from the backbenches he urged it to take decisive, warlike action. On 28 May he demanded that saddles *en route* from the London-based Company of Armourers, Gunsmiths and Saddlers to the king at York should be seized, and that a volunteer force be raised to go to Ireland. Four days later, on 1 June, he proposed that two ships be sent to guard the mouth of the River Tyne to prevent foreign aid being sent to the king in the north.

What is especially striking and revealing about the strength of Cromwell's belief in the necessity of military action is his decision to leave London, probably about 10 August, for Cambridge to organise local resistance to those who supported the king. With his brother-in-law, Valentine Walton, and a small troop of soldiers, he seized the stock of arms and ammunition ('the magazine') in Cambridge Castle, and also forcibly intercepted an armed escort that was taking money and plate from the University of Cambridge to the king at York. The Civil War had not yet officially begun (the king did not set up his standard at Nottingham until 22 August) and it is difficult to exaggerate the risks Cromwell ran of being accused of robbery and treason if the rebellion against the king had fizzled out, as it might well have done. What is remarkable about Cromwell on the eve of the war is that he did not share the uncertainties about the rights and wrongs of resistance to the king, and the consequent indecision of many of his countrymen. A week after the official start of the war he raised a troop of horse at Huntingdon, with his son-in-law, John Desborough, as quartermaster, and, after briefly returning to Westminster, he left with his small eighty-strong cavalry force to join the main parliamentary field army under the earl of Essex on the campaign that included the indecisive battle of Edgehill, fought on 22 October 1642.

Despite the many unknown facts about Cromwell's early career we can presume that when the Civil War began he was as fully committed to fighting against the king as anyone else in England. Moreover, his main concern was the defence of parliament. When he later said 'religion was not the thing at the first contested for' he meant that the attainment of religious liberty was not the main reason he fought for parliament at the beginning of the war.[25] In September 1644 he wrote that 'I profess I could never satisfy myself as to the justness of this War, but from the authority of the Parliament to maintain itself in its rights; and in this Cause I hope to approve myself an honest man and single-hearted'.[26] He believed that when parliament's liberties were secured then religious liberty of conscience within a national Church would inevitably follow. The Civil War if anything strengthened Cromwell's determination to continue the struggle to secure these ends. But what happened during the war caused him to doubt for the first time whether securing parliamentary liberties was an automatic guarantee of the completion of the godly reformation. During the course of the war Cromwell was to realise that the cause for which he fought was not as clear-cut as he had thought when he ambushed the Royalist escort leaving Cambridge on the Great North Road in August 1642.

. . .

NOTES AND REFERENCES

1. H.N. Brailsford, *The Levellers and the English Revolution* (Cresset Press, 1961), p. 297.
2. James Heath, *Flagellum, or the Life and Death, Birth and Burial of Oliver Cromwell, the Late Usurper* (London, 1663), p. 7.
3. *Ibid.*, p. 8.
4. Abbott, vol. IV, p. 493.
5. John Morrill, 'The making of Oliver Cromwell' in John Morrill, ed., *Oliver Cromwell and the English Revolution* (Longman, 1990), p. 28.
6. Brian Quintrell, 'Oliver Cromwell and the distraint of knighthood', *Bulletin of the Institute of Historical Research*, **57**, 1984.
7. *Calendar of State Papers Domestic 1631–33*, p. 501.
8. See, for example, Heath's scurrilous comment that 'they say that the Lord Protector's Instrument is found under my Lady Lambert's petticoat', Heath, *Flagellum*, p. 128.
9. Abbott, vol. III, p. 452.
10. Abbott, vol. I, pp. 96–7.
11. Abbott, vol. I, pp. 64–5.
12. A.N.B. Cotton, 'John Dillingham, journalist of the middle group', *English Historical Review*, **93**, 1978, p. 821.
13. For the 'godly' see P. Collinson, *The Religion of Protestants: the Church in England 1559–1625* (Oxford University Press, 1982) and E. Duffy, 'The godly and the multitude in Stuart England', *The Seventeenth Century*, I, 1986.
14. Abbott, vol. I, p. 124.
15. Abbott, vol. I, p. 136.
16. Abbott, vol. I, p. 128.
17. Morrill, 'The making of Oliver Cromwell', in Morrill, *Cromwell*, pp. 43–5.
18. Abbott, vol. I, p. 69.

19. Abbott, vol. I, p. 123.
20. Abbott, vol. I, p. 132.
21. W.H.Coates (ed.), *The Journal of Sir Simonds D'Ewes from the First Recess of the Long Parliament to the Withdrawal of the King from London* (Yale University Press, 1942), p. 40.
22. Abbott, vol. II, p. 198.
23. V.F. Snow and A.S. Young (eds), *The Private Journals of the Long Parliament*, 7 March – 1 June 1642 (Yale University Press, 1987), p. 8.
24. *Ibid.*, p. 104.
25. Abbott, vol. III, p. 586 (speech of 22 January 1655).
26. Abbott, vol. I, p. 292 (letter of 5 September 1644).

Chapter 2

CROMWELL AND THE CIVIL WAR (1642–46)

The Civil War shaped Oliver Cromwell's political outlook in two major ways. First, it confirmed the belief he had already adopted by 1642: that the war was a just one and that he and the king's opponents had God's support. Even though, as will be seen, his military career before the battle of Marston Moor on 2 July 1644 does not merit the excessive praise it has often been given, Cromwell did help to prevent eastern England from falling wholly into Royalist hands. He interpreted this limited success as clear evidence of God's blessing. Moreover, especially after the battle of Marston Moor, his self-confidence increased to such an extent that first others, and then Cromwell himself, came to believe that he and the army had a divinely ordained mission to win the war and bring about a godly reformation. Thus one major effect of the Civil War on Cromwell was not only to give him greater confidence in himself but also a growing reputation outside as well as inside the army. This enabled him to play a much more important political role than ever before. At the start of the Civil War Cromwell was a political nonentity; within a couple of years of its outbreak he had been transformed into someone who, in the words of Bulstrode Whitelocke, 'began to appear in the world'.[1]

The second effect of the Civil War on Cromwell was to shatter his political innocence. As the war developed he realised that not all his wartime allies shared either his desire to prosecute the war wholeheartedly or his hopes that the outcome of the king's defeat would be godly reformation. Increasingly he found himself at odds, not only with Royalist troops, but with 'enemies within' the parliamentary alliance. The sense of shock and disillusionment he felt at this discovery forced him to abandon his naive belief that all he needed to do was to prosecute the war effectively in defence of parliamentary liberties. Instead he came to see that, if the war was to result in a godly reformation, it would have to be fought in the political arena as well as on the battlefield. Cromwell's experience of war gave him the growing self-confidence necessary to fight Royalists on the battlefield and also the knowledge that he had to use his new political reputation to help to defeat the 'enemies within' the parliamentary cause at Westminster. 'Religion [i.e. religious liberty] was not the thing at the first contested for', but, according to Cromwell, during the Civil War 'God brought it to that issue at last.'[2]

. . .

BEFORE MARSTON MOOR

Cromwell does not seem to have been given an identifiably distinct military role until early in January 1643, when he was promoted from colonel to captain, detached from the earl of Essex's army and sent from London to East Anglia to support Lord Grey of Warke, the head of the newly formed Eastern Association, which consisted initially of Norfolk, Suffolk, Essex, Cambridgeshire and Hertfordshire, one of a number of associations of counties established by parliament in the first winter of the war in an attempt to secure regional co-operation in its war effort. Cromwell's role in the Eastern Association became more important when in April 1643 Grey of Warke departed with 5,000 horse and foot to join Essex's army in the Thames Valley, placing much of the responsibility for the defence of the Eastern Association on Cromwell. His task was two-fold: to suppress opposition to and galvanise support for the parliamentary cause within the associated counties, and to defend the territorial integrity of the region against Royalist attacks from outside its borders mounted by local Royalist garrisons (especially a powerful one at Newark in Lincolnshire) and by a major Royalist army led by the earl of Newcastle, which was slowly marching southwards through Yorkshire towards the nothern borders of the Eastern Association.

Cromwell had some success in both these tasks. He set

energetically to work, with a few other local militant activ-
ists, trying to dispel the prevailing mood in the eastern
counties, which ranged from apathy and prevarication to
outright Royalism. On his way from London to Cambridge
in January 1643 he arrested the sheriff of Hertfordshire as
a suspected Royalist and he prevented the proclamation of
the Royalist commission of array, which authorised the raising of troops in the king's name. Moreover, when he got to
Cambridge he worked with the parliamentary committee
there, attempting to collect money from the associated
counties and initiating moves towards inter-county collaboration at a meeting of representatives from Suffolk, Cambridgeshire, Norfolk and Essex held at Bury St Edmunds
on 4 February. Then in March he and his troops swept
through Norfolk, via Norwich, Lowestoft and King's Lynn,
intimidating and arresting as Royalists and papists those
who refused to commit themselves to the parliamentary
cause. Many of these, like the gentlemen who opposed
Eastern Association forces at King's Lynn in August 1643,
may have been genuinely uncommitted neutrals. But to
Cromwell who feared (as he said in a letter of 26 January
1643) that 'the Papists in Norfolk are solicited to rise presently'[3] the distinction between a Royalist and a neutral was
not one that at this stage he was prepared to recognise. At
times he used very firm measures to maintain parliamentary control. His appointment as military governor of Ely
in July 1643 (after a Royalist uprising there in May) was
part of a policy of establishing garrisons in key towns in
East Anglia which had some success in intimidating the
population into submission to parliamentary authority.

Cromwell also had some success in establishing the
northern frontier of the Eastern Association at the River
Nene against the strong Royalist garrison at Newark. This
involved his first recorded experiences of siege warfare at
Crowland Abbey, near Peterborough (25–28 April 1643), as
part of his attempt to clear armed Royalists out of the Eastern Association heartland. Later in the year Cromwell was
also active on the battlefield, supporting the parliamentary
commander in Lincolnshire, Sir Francis Willoughby of Par-
ham, as the main Royalist army under Newcastle advanced
southwards from Yorkshire, threatening the northern border of the Eastern Association counties. On 24 July Crom-

well took Burleigh House, near Stamford in Lincolnshire, and was successfully involved in skirmishes with Royalist troops at Grantham (May), Gainsborough (July) and Winceby (October), fighting a desperate rearguard action against outriders from Newcastle's main army.

None of Cromwell's military victories in 1643 were of major importance in the wider context of the Civil War. They were skirmishes rather than full-scale battles; at best all they succeeded in doing was slowing down the southward march of Newcastle's army. But, limited though his military successes were, they were seized on by London parliamentary newspapers, such as the *Parliament Scout*, and made much of in a desperate propaganda attempt to counter fears of an imminent outright Royalist victory, so contributing to the emergence of an image, which was to be fully developed later by contemporaries and historians, depicting Cromwell as parliament's saviour. It is important not to accept that image uncritically. In this and later chapters it will be shown that Cromwell's military career during and after 1643 was by no means one of unqualified success.

There are, however, features of Cromwell's image as a soldier presented at the time and since that are well-substantiated by evidence from 1643, and which (if not all of them are unique) are at least unusual among officers of both sides in the Civil War. Four of these stand out. First, Cromwell had a very close relationship with the men under his command. This was based on a combination of tight military discipline with frequent displays of concern for their well-being. From the very beginning, newspaper reports commented on Cromwell's strictness towards soldiers who deserted or misbehaved. In May 1643 *Special Passages* contained a report that in Cromwell's regiment 'no man swears but he pays his twelve-pence; if he be drunk, he is set in the stocks or worse; if one calls the other "Roundhead" he is cashiered: insomuch that the countries where they come leap for joy of them, and come in and join with them. How happy were it if all the forces were thus disciplined.'[4] Yet Cromwell supported his soldiers when they were not being paid properly (as will be seen), or when he thought they were being treated unfairly, as in September 1643, when one of his officers, Captain Margery, was accused of taking horses from civilians without due cause.

27

Second, contemporaries agreed that from his earliest military engagements Cromwell exercised an unusually high degree of discipline on, as well as off, the battlefield. Unlike many other cavalry commanders, Cromwell took his cavalry into battle in a close, tight formation, and having broken through the enemy's ranks did not allow his men to chase those in flight for plunder, but instead regrouped his forces into a tight formation to attack the enemy still on the battlefield from the rear. At a minor skirmish at Gainsborough in July 1643 Cromwell's cavalry successfully followed that manoeuvre, which it was to repeat in later battles with more momentous consequences.

Third, as he recruited more men in 1643 (within a year after the outbreak of the war the men under his command had risen from one troop to ten troops of about eighty men each) he 'raised such men as had the fear of God before them, and made some conscience of what they did'.[5] Many times in 1643 he boasted of the godly qualities of his soldiers. 'I have a lovely company', he wrote to Oliver St John on 11 September. 'They are no Anabaptists, they are honest sober Christians: they expect to be used as men.'[6] 'Mine (though some have stigmatised them with the name of Anabaptists) are honest men, such as fear God', he wrote to Sir Francis Barrington a month later.[7] Cromwell was not the only Civil War commander to endeavour to recruit godly soldiers. The earl of Manchester, soon to be his senior commander in the Eastern Association army, for a time recruited to his army 'honest men though differing in judgement to what I profess'.[8] But he was making a radical departure from the normal practice of promoting men primarily on account of their social rank, and was undoubtedly implicitly threatening the existing social order. However, Cromwell did not see what he was doing in that light. The oft-quoted statement in Cromwell's letter to the Suffolk parliamentary county committee of 29 August 1643 might seem to suggest otherwise: 'I had rather have a plain russet-coated captain that knows what he fights for, and loves what he knows, than that which you call a gentleman and is nothing else.' However, Cromwell added a sentence that is not often quoted, which puts a different gloss on his attitude: 'I honour a gentleman that is so indeed.'[9] Gentility was not a bar to promotion in his regiments (many of his officers were gentlemen), but godly commitment in his officers was as important to him as gentility.

Above all, however, what marks out Cromwell the soldier from the very beginning of his career is his constant attribution of military victories to God's help. In 1643 even a minor skirmish, such as that at Grantham in May, was seen as 'a glorious victory' won 'by God's providence', and he was even convinced that victories achieved by fellow commanders, for instance, Sir Thomas Fairfax's at Wakefield (also in May), were 'a great mercy of God'.[10] When he first took to the battlefield against the Royalists Cromwell was already a self-confident commander of an army, characterised more than most Civil War armies by discipline and zealous commitment to the cause of parliament. Later these features were to help him overcome his inexperience and to win remarkable military victories. However, judging by what happened to him in 1643, these qualities alone were not a guarantee of victory on the battlefield.

Indeed, Cromwell's faith in God's support was sorely tested in 1643. As the year wore on, he became increasingly panic-stricken at the military failures suffered by his fellow commanders and himself. What successes he had were restricted to victories within the territory of the Eastern Association. Whenever he tried to participate in wider, more ambitious strategies, involving collaboration with other regional parliamentary forces, his experience was one of total failure. Early in May 1643, for example, the principal parliamentary armies in the East Midlands under Lord Grey of Groby and Sir John Gell, the Lincolnshire parliamentary regiments under Willoughby and Cromwell's forces failed (despite the orders of the earl of Essex) to combine to prevent a convoy of ammunition from Queen Henrietta Maria, being sent south to Oxford. (Henrietta Maria had landed with foreign supplies of men, money and arms at Bridlington earlier in the year.)

Cromwell was angry that Lord Grey failed to meet him at Stamford, 'according to our agreement; fearing the exposing of Leicester to the [Royalist] forces of Mr Hastings and some other troops drawing that way. Believe it, it were better, in my poor opinion, Leicester were not than there should not be an immediate taking of the field to accomplish the common end.'[11] But what Cromwell was not always ready to admit was that he himself was far from blameless in the failure to effect collaborative action to 'accomplish the common end'. When the regional commanders (including Sir John Hotham, and Miles Corbet, as well as Grey, Gell and Cromwell) did finally meet at Nottingham at the end of May and the beginning of June 1643, their joint forces stayed put in a state of paralysis for two weeks. On 2 June Cromwell and his fellow commanders wrote to Fairfax explaining their failure to march against Newcastle's massive army, and the best excuse they could devise was a blatantly false one: that they 'had certain intelligence of the state of my Lord Newcastle's army, so weak and in such distraction'.[12] The *real* reasons for their inaction were quarrels amongst themselves (Hotham was soon to be arrested for being a traitor to the parliamentary cause) and dire financial problems. As yet parliamentary troops largely relied on local subscriptions for money; not surprisingly these were inadequate. The result was that, when Cromwell appealed to the mayor of Colchester from Nottingham for money to be sent to him, his infantry and dragoon regiments were 'ready to mutiny',[13] and he had to borrow money from merchants in the town to prevent this from happening. Not surprisingly, another Royalist convoy, led by the queen herself, got through from Yorkshire to Oxford unscathed. What is more, later in July, Cromwell failed to obey Essex's instructions to meet him in the Midlands at Stony Stratford to help him defend Oxford.

By the summer of 1643 Cromwell was in no position to provide military support elsewhere. His position was as dire as that of many other parliamentary commanders. At about this time the western parliamentary army under Sir William Waller suffered a series of defeats at the hands of Sir Ralph Hopton and Prince Rupert in the West Country, and the earl of Essex's army was in deadlock with Royalist forces in the Thames Valley around Oxford. Cromwell himself was faced with a major threat from the earl of Newcastle's army, which was poised to invade the heartland of the Eastern Association: and on 28 July, despite Cromwell's successful cavalry charge there, it took Gainsborough from Willoughby, and by the middle of August Newcastle was in control of the whole of Lincolnshire. Cromwell's letters at this time are tense and urgent, verging on panic. 'See', he wrote to the Cambridgeshire committee on 6 August 1643, 'how sadly your affairs stand. It's no longer disputing, but out instantly all you can. Raise all your hands . . . get up what volunteers you can; haste your horses.' 'Lord Newcastle will advance into your bowels', he told the deputy lieutenants of Essex graphically on the same day, at the same time castigating them for allowing Essex's troops to return home: 'Is this the way to save a kingdom?'[14]

For Cromwell the answer was clearly 'no', and perhaps he was already groping towards a political solution to the problems of lack of money and localism that contributed to the disastrous state of the parliamentary war effort at this time. There is, though, no direct evidence that Cromwell collaborated with those who at Westminster early in August pushed through parliament ordinances which began to reorganise the Eastern Association by appointing the earl of Manchester as its major-general and empowering Manchester and the parliamentary committees of the Association to conscript up to 20,000 men. Nor were there any signs that these measures had an impact on the fortunes of the war in eastern England. Indeed, Cromwell's letters during the next three months became, if anything, even more panic-stricken. 'The force [Manchester's] will fall if some help not', he wrote to Oliver St John on 11 September. 'Weak counsels and weak actings undo all. Send at once or come or all will be lost, if God help not.'[15] Moreover, he became increasingly despondent: 'he wept', wrote an Essex gentleman reporting Cromwell's first meeting with Fairfax in September, 'when he came to Boston and found no moneys for him from Essex and other counties'.[16] By the end of the year Cromwell's troops were again reported to be (as they had been in the spring) on the verge of mutiny.

This was the desperate situation which forced Cromwell and his senior commander, Manchester, to leave the battlefront and go to London (Cromwell was there from 18 January to mid-February 1644) to work for a political solution to the military problem. At Westminster, however, they found that not everyone sympathised with their plight. By this stage deep divisions had opened up among civilian parliamentarians about the conduct of the war. Conservative 'peace group' MPs, of whom Denzil Holles was the most vocal, had given up any hopes they might have had in

1642 of winning a decisive military victory, and they were now pressing for the conclusion of a speedy peace treaty with the king and, in the meantime, for a defensive war strategy. There were, however, MPs at Westminster (labelled by historians 'war group' and 'middle group' men) who maintained their initial conviction that the king must be defeated militarily before meaningful peace negotiations could begin. John Pym, who in 1643 had pushed through parliament new war taxation, administrative reorganisation and an alliance with the Scots, was now dead. But his mantle in the Commons had been taken on by Oliver St John, working with a group of peers including Lords Saye and Sele and Wharton, with whom Cromwell had been loosely associated before the war. It was natural, therefore, that Cromwell in 1644 should resume these contacts as a means of securing parliamentary measures designed to strengthen the eastern parliamentary army. However, Cromwell now played a much more central, and astute, role than he had in 1641–42 in the successful campaign that secured for Manchester more money and greater control over regional army commanders in eastern England. On 17 January he moved in the Commons the acceptance of a financial ordinance increasing by 50 per cent monthly assessments levied on the individual counties of the Association and putting the money under the control of a central committee, chaired by Manchester, at Cambridge. And on 22 January Cromwell made a scathing speech in the Commons, attacking Willoughby's inefficiency as a general and his appointment of 'loose and profane commanders'.[17] Unlike Cromwell's interventions in parliamentary proceedings before the war, these were skilfully timed to coincide with a co-ordinated political campaign masterminded by Cromwell's senior civilian parliamentary allies and denoted a surer sense of political touch, as well as a closer proximity to those directing political events than ever before. Cromwell's promotion in January to Lieutenant-General of the Eastern Association, Manchester's second-in-command, and his appointment to the newly established Committee of Both Kingdoms at Westminster in February confirmed his new, more important military and political status among the king's parliamentary opponents on the eve of his first great military victory.

. . .

AFTER MARSTON MOOR

Cromwell's assessment of the battle of Marston Moor on 2 July 1644 as a 'great victory . . . such as the like never was since this war began' is correct.[18] But the battle was not a turning point in the history of the English Civil War after which a parliamentary victory was inevitable. Contemporaries would have been astonished that anyone should have ever suggested that this was the case. Immediately after the victory at Marston Moor the English parliamentarians and their Scottish allies (who had formally joined the war against the king in the previous autumn after making a treaty with the parliamentarians known as the Solemn League and Convenant) were euphoric. But this mood rapidly changed during the mext few months as parliament's two main armies suffered severe setbacks. Essex's army was decimated at Lostwithiel in Cornwall in August, and Manchester's (as will be seen) performed badly against the king's army in Berkshire in the autumn. The battle of Marston Moor, however, was a watershed in the career of Oliver Cromwell in two major respects.

The first stems from the fact that Cromwell believed that he and his cavalry had won the battle and that his allies, Fairfax, Manchester, Leven and the Scots, had played a relatively insignificant (at best) supporting part in the victory. This is a judgement that receives some support from recent assessments of the battle by military historians.[19] Remarkably, given that this was Cromwell's first experience of holding a major command in a full-scale battle, his control of his cavalry troopers was disciplined and close (replicating on a much grander scale the tactics he had used fighting at Gainsborough in the previous year). 'We never charged but we routed the enemy. The left wing, which I commanded, being our own horse, saving a few Scots in our rear, beat all the Prince's horse', he boasted with some justice, since the ability of his cavalry to re-group after the initial charge enabled him to go to the rescue of Sir Thomas Fairfax's cavalry and to join up with the infantry regiments of the Eastern Association army under Major-General Lawrence Crawford, to bring about a victory over Prince Rupert and Newcastle, while his senior commanders, Manchester and Leven, had fled the battlefield. Not surprisingly, his key role in the victory gave him a much bigger boost of confidence than ever before and confirmed his belief that his actions and the cause for which he fought had divine sanction. 'Truly England and the Church of God hath had a great favour from the Lord . . . God made them as stubble to our swords'.[20] It also gave him a tremendous contemporary reputation. Not surprisingly, Cromwell's political allies at Westminster echoed his providential interpretation of what had happened and of his own key role. A pamphlet published in 1654, *Vindiciae Veritatis*, which was probably written in 1646 by Lord Saye and Sele, proclaimed in Cromwellian phraseology that 'it hath pleased God to use, as instruments under him, Cromwell . . . to give the turn, win the day, and to take the Victorie out of the enemies hands. This was the Lord's doing.' This image of Cromwell, moreover, was generally accepted after Marston Moor. The newspaper *Perfect Diurnal* on 18 March 1645 referred to Cromwell as 'one of the Saviours (as God hath miraculously manifested him to be) of this Israel'.[21] It was not only Cromwell and his friends who came to see him as a man with a divine mission to save the English nation, as Moses had rescued the Israelites from Egyptian oppression.

Marston Moor not only propelled Cromwell to a national military and political reputation: it also awakened Cromwell to the fact that not all his allies shared his commitment to religious liberty of conscience. Until the siege of York, in May and June 1644, there is very little evidence that he had any suspicion that this was so. When, earlier in the year, Cromwell learned that Lawrence Crawford, his colleague in the army of the Eastern Association, had disciplined two men for their religious beliefs, he appealed to Crawford to be more tolerant: even though a man might be an Anabaptist, he wrote to Crawford, 'shall that render him incapable to serve the public? . . . Sir, the State in choosing men to serve them, takes no notice of their opinions, if they be willing faithfully to serve them, that satisfies'.[22] These were views that to this point Cromwell shared with Manchester, who, when he began recruiting the new-style army of the Eastern Association in the autumn of 1643, selected, as has been seen, 'many honest men, though differing in judgement to what I profess'. John Lilburne was one who was attracted by this liberal attitude, and he later said that he left Essex's army to join the Eastern Association forces of 'my then two darlings', Manchester and Cromwell. Before Marston Moor, Manchester was not averse to accepting Independents in his army, and Cromwell at the same time supported Presbyterians, like Colonel Edward King, whose promotion he secured to the command of the Eastern Association forces in Lincolnshire. Moreover, Cromwell himself appointed at least thirteen Scottish Presbyterian officers to his army, and he took the Presbyterian Covenant in February 1644.

What caused Cromwell after the battle of Marston Moor to be much more wary than hitherto of co-operating with Presbyterians? Partly it was a reaction to the intolerant views of the Scottish Presbyterian officers he talked to during the siege of York. In an attempt to counter these he promoted a petition at York favouring toleration; and it may be that the mission by Sir Henry Vane junior to York in June, which was once wrongly thought to have been part of a plot to depose the king,[23] was an attempt to support Cromwell's efforts to get Scottish assurances on toleration. But it was the effect of his victory at Marston Moor, which he saw as a judgement by God in favour of his 'godly party', which, above all, prompted Cromwell to take more determined action to oppose those with intolerant views. After the battle he attempted to get Crawford, whom he had clashed with earlier in the year, cashiered from the army, and Manchester had to order both of his junior officers to appear before the Committee of Both Kingdoms in London in an attempt to settle the quarrel. It was also alleged by the Scot, Robert Baillie, that Cromwell and his 'party' in the weeks after Marston Moor purged some Presbyterians from his regiments, intending to 'frame the whole army to their devotion. . . . This hes [sic] been the Independents great plott.'[24]

But the change in Cromwell's attitude after Marston Moor cannot be fully explained without taking account of Manchester's reactions to what had happened. Unlike Cromwell, Manchester reacted to the battle and its aftermath with great alarm, caused by the fear that a decisive victory over the king would lead to religious disputes (as was already happening in his own army) and a threat to social order. As a result, Cromwell became increasingly critical of his senior commander, whom he feared was now unwilling 'to have this war prosecuted unto full victory'. Cromwell also alleged that Manchester had 'a design or desire to have it ended by accommodation and that on some such terms to which it might be disadvantageous to bring the king too low', and that he was seeking a settlement with the king on the basis of intolerant Presbyterianism.[25] Certainly, after the battle Manchester was no longer as effective a general as he had been. The collaboration of Manchester's Eastern Association army and Sir William Waller's western army against the Royalist forces commanded by the king in Berkshire ended in disaster at battles at Newbury and Donnington Castle in October 1644. The parliamentary forces made tactical errors and, at the Council of War's *post mortem*, Manchester's conduct was severely criticised by Waller and Cromwell. The consequence was that the parliamentary war effort faced an even bigger crisis than at the beginning of the year, and the quarrelling army commanders were again forced to return to London to try to resolve it politically.

Cromwell's three-month stay in London from the end of November 1644 until the beginning of March 1645 proved to be a vital stage in his education in the art of politics. Shortly after his return to London on 25 November he made a long indictment in the House of Commons of Manchester's 'averseness to action' in the latest phase of the war. However, as in January 1644, he was not acting alone: as before, his parliamentary intervention was part of a concerted political campaign masterminded by powerful political allies. By this stage, the divisions among Westminster politicians that had existed in January were now, if anything, wider and more bitter than ever. Cromwell's political allies with whom he had co-operated effectively in January now faced formidable opposition. By the end of the year their 'peace group' enemies had gained the support of the Scots, who began to negotiate with the king for a settlement on the basis of Scottish Presbyterianism in the Church. They had also been joined by the earl of Essex, who (like Manchester) was driven by a desire to halt what he saw as the dangerously radical religious views of Cromwell and his allies inside and outside the army. This new political alignment makes it highly likely that Cromwell's attack on Manchester was part of a political campaign, conducted by Oliver St John and his aristocratic allies, such as Lords Saye and Sele and Wharton, against Essex and the Scots, as well as Manchester.

It is not surprising in these circumstances that Cromwell's indictment of Manchester provoked a sharp retaliation. Three days later in the Lords, Manchester delivered a set of four principal counter-charges against Cromwell: (1) that his junior officer should share the blame for the recent military debacles in Berkshire; (2) that he had shown 'animosities against the Scottish nation' and had said 'he could as soon draw his sword against them as against any in the king's army'; (3) that 'he desires to have none in the army but such as were of the Independent judgement'; and (4) that 'his expressions were sometimes against the Nobillitie; that he hoped to live to see never a Nobleman in England, and he loved such better then others because they did not love lords'.[26] Given the highly charged political atmosphere in which these allegations were made, it is likely that they were exaggerated. But only the last one has little substance and is difficult to accept, given that Cromwell's major political allies were noblemen, together with his later defence of the House of Lords in 1649. Cromwell, however, had done enough in recent months to suggest that the charges of hostility to the Scots and Presbyterians in the army were not without foundation. Moreover, it is likely that Manchester had not been the only indecisive general on the Berkshire campaign. One of the principal reasons for the failure of the parliamentary forces at Newbury and Donnington was the poor showing of Cromwell's cavalry. In great contrast to its achievements at Marston Moor and later at Naseby and Langport, Cromwell's cavalry had allowed the king's forces to escape at Newbury and had stood by while Donnington Castle was relieved and the Royalists recovered their abandoned artillery unscathed. At the time Cromwell had excused his failure to act on the grounds of the exhaustion of the horses which 'are so spent, so harassed out by hard duty, that they will fall down under their riders if you command them; you may have their skins but you can have no service'.[27] He also admitted on 9 December that 'I must acknowledge myself guilty of oversights, so I know they can rarely be avoided in military matters.'[28] But Manchester had little difficulty in raising suspicions at Westminster that there was more to Cromwell's inaction than exhaustion and 'oversights'. At a meeting at Essex's house on 1 December, Essex and Holles met representatives of the Scots to discuss the possibility of impeaching Cromwell, 'that darling of the sectaries'. It was decided not to proceed, because of Cromwell's now considerable military and political reputation – 'the interest Cromwell had in the parliament and army' was, they decided, far too strong – but the attack on Cromwell was pressed home in the House of Lords during the next few days.

On the face of it Cromwell's escape from this dangerous political crisis and triumphant emergence shortly afterwards as a key commander of the New Model parliamentary army was remarkable and substantiates a picture of a Machiavellian Cromwell, a master of political guile, who manipulated events to secure his self-advancement. (His political opponents were thrown temporarily into disarray, and Essex as well as Manchester was forced out of the army.) It is, however, a picture that fades away on closer inspection, leaving only one element of it intact: what is certain is that by this stage Cromwell had become an adept master of the art of politics. He survived the political crisis because he had powerful allies at Westminster, because he was lucky and because of his political surefootedness.

Cromwell's survival began when, in a Commons' speech on 9 December 1644, he floated the idea of a Self-Denying Ordinance, which would make it illegal for any MP to hold an army command. This was a brilliant political ploy to unite the nation and destroy the campaign against him. It was, however, not devised by Cromwell but by his parliamentary allies. Significantly, Saye and Sele introduced the same resolution in the Lords on the same day. Its call to MPs to lay down their army commands and not 'perpetually continue themselves in grandeur' was an appeal to a powerful Puritan ideal of self-denial, as well as the chauvinist sentiments of those with 'true English hearts, and zealous affections towards the general weal of our Mother Country'.[29] It was also designed to secure the support of

MPs committed to both sides in the current political controversy, who could support it as a means of ejecting their respective opponents from the army. As far as Cromwell's continuing military career was concerned, the most that he and his allies could have hoped for is that his exemption from the Self-Denying Ordinance would be secured as part of a deal in which Essex would also be allowed to retain his army command. Essex's exemption, however, was voted down narrowly by 100 votes to 93 on 17 December, and this must have seemed to have signalled the end of Cromwell's military career when the ordinance came into effect. Cromwell continued to play a key role in the political events that led to its successful passage through parliament, as well as to the reconstruction of the army, following the departure of the old aristocratic generals: in January 1645 he was teller with Sir John Evelyn in a vote in favour of Fairfax becoming Lord General of the army, and he attended most of the meetings of the Commons' committee that devised the structure of the new army, amalgamating the three existing parliamentary armies previously commanded by Waller, Essex and Manchester into one New Model Army. As is well known, Cromwell subsequently escaped the provisions of the Self-Denying Ordinance by a series of grants of temporary exemptions in order to enable him to serve with Waller in the West of England during March to early April, and around Oxford and in the Midlands with Fairfax thereafter. But it is highly unlikely that he could ever have foreseen that this would be the eventual outcome when he rose to speak in the Commons a few months earlier on 9 December 1644.

On 10 June, with the New Model Army threatened by Rupert's army, victorious after its sack of Leicester on 1 May, the Commons approved Fairfax's petition for Cromwell's appointment to the post of his second-in-command, as Lieutenant General of Horse, which had remained vacant since the establishment of the army. Four days later the New Model Army won a crushing victory over Rupert at Naseby and a month later an equally decisive victory at Langport, the last major battle of the war. In both these battles, as at Marston Moor, the role of Cromwell's disciplined cavalry was decisive, reinforcing the view that Cromwell's main strength as a soldier during the Civil War was as a cavalry commander rather than as a general in overall command of the movement of armies on and off the battlefield.

The importance of Cromwell's return to the army during the last phase of the Civil War (he spent all but a few days away from London between March 1645 and June 1646) is that it brought him yet more evidence of God's blessing. His letters written immediately after victories in both minor skirmishes and major battles alike ring with the same providential message. After his forces had taken Bletchingdon House near Oxford in April 1645 he wrote to the Committee of Both Kingdoms that 'this was the mercy of God . . . God brought them [the enemy] to our hands when we looked not for them. . . . His mercy appears in this also that I did much doubt the storming of the house, it being strong and well manned, and I having few dragoons . . . and yet we got it.'[30] 'Sir', he enthused in his battle report on Naseby in June 1645, 'this is none other than the hand of God, and to Him alone belongs the glory.'[31] A month later after the New Model Army's victory at Langport (Long Sutton), his language was ecstatic: 'Thus you see what the Lord hath wrought for us. Can any creature ascribe anything to itself? Now can we give all the glory to God, and desire all may do so, for it is all due unto Him! Thus you have Long Sutton mercy added to Naseby mercy. And to see this, is it not to see the face of God?'[32] These were the 'chains of providences' he was to look to for inspiration in later life at times when he was caught in the tangled jungle of political intrigue. Now, too, they gave him a sense of confidence, as well as relief that, after the political in-fighting of the past few months, he was again able to see the struggle in uncomplicated terms of right and wrong. As he marched westwards into Devon, early in 1646, his optimism led him to see himself as the leader of an army of liberation: 'We are come', he told recruits at Totnes on 24 January 1646, 'to set you, if possible, at liberty from your taskmasters, and by settling Peace, bring Plenty to you again.'[33]

During these last military campaigns of the Civil War, too, the demands for 'liberty' Cromwell forwarded to Westminster became more strident and he was more than ever anxious to remind MPs that the 'liberty' he had in mind was religious liberty as well as the protection of parliamentary liberties. 'Honest men served you faithfully in this action', he wrote to MPs after Naseby. 'He that ventures his life for the liberty of his country, I wish he trust God for the liberty of his conscience, and for the liberty he fights for.'[34] 'We look for no compulsion [in religion]', he wrote after the victory at Bristol in September 1645, 'but that of light and reason'.[35] Increasingly, too, his demands for reformation became identified with the army, and expressed (as in the Naseby letter above) in terms that echoed the post-war hopes of soldiers after the First World War in 1918 that there would be created 'a land fit for heroes to live in'. As has been noted, Cromwell had been concerned from the beginning of the war about the material welfare of his soldiers. During the war these bonds between Cromwell and his men, born out of shared experiences of living together in stressful conditions, were strengthened. At Langport he wrote to parliament on behalf of John Lilburne, who was owed arrears of pay for the time he had served with Cromwell in the Eastern Association army. 'Truly it is a grief to see men ruin themselves through their affection and faithfulness to the public. . . . It would be an honour to the Parliament and an encouragement to those that faithfully serve them, if provisions were made for the comfortable subsistence of those who have lost all for them.'[36] These were sentiments that later in his career led Cromwell to despair at times about the sincerity of parliament's concern for religious liberty and for the welfare of the army.

However, this was not the case at the end of the war. It is true that before Cromwell returned to Westminster there was clear evidence that many MPs were opposed to his demands for religious liberty. Significantly, when Cromwell's Naseby and Bristol letters were printed by parliamentary order his demands for religious liberty were censored. Cromwell's political allies at Westminster printed the offending sections privately and Lord Saye and Sele published a defence of Cromwell against the charges made by conservative MPs that religious liberty would open the floodgates to social and political radicalism. Cromwell appears, however, to have been unaffected by these political divisions. During the siege of Bristol, in September 1645, he wrote a series of letters which indicate that his main aim then was to rebuild the unity of the king's opponents that had been disrupted during the war and especially by the traumatic quarrels of the previous winter. In his letter to the Scottish commander, the earl of Leven, on 2 September, he attempted to paper over the divisions between the Scots and English that had developed in the aftermath of Marston Moor. 'We hope the unity of spirit [between the two countries] shall be the surest bond of peace', he wrote.[37] Similarly, in a letter to parliament of 14 September rejoicing at the capture of Bristol, he stressed the unity among English Protestants that had not been apparent in recent months: 'Presbyterians, Independents, all had the same spirit of faith and prayer . . . they agree here, know no names of difference: pity it should be otherwise anywhere. All that believe have the real unity.'[38] Significantly too, he reasserted his belief that the godly cause and the parliamentary cause were one. In a letter he wrote (with Fairfax) to the sheriff and gentry of Cornwall on 8 September, he urged them to be 'sensible of the interest of Religion, and of the rights and liberties of yourselves and the rest of the people of England, of which [he concluded] the power and authority of Parliaments hath been in former ages and is ever like to be (under God) the best conservatory and support'.[39] Thus Cromwell returned to London at the end of the war still convinced that the mission given him by God and the demands of the army could be achieved by a parliamentary settlement.

·   ·   ·

NOTES AND REFERENCES

1. Bulstrode Whitelocke, *Memorials of the English Affairs* (Oxford, 1852, 4 vols) vol. I, p. 209.
2. Abbott, vol. III, p. 586.
3. Abbott, vol. I, p. 211.
4. Abbott, vol. I, p. 231.
5. Abbott, vol. IV, p. 471 (speech of 13 April 1657).
6. Abbott, vol. I, p. 258.
7. Abbott, vol. I, p. 264.
8. *Letter from the Earl of Manchester to the House of Lords* (Camden Miscellany, vol. 8, 1853), item 5.
9. Abbott, vol. I, p. 256.

10. Abbott, vol. I, pp. 230, 231.
11. Abbott, vol. I, p. 228.
12. Abbott, vol. I, p. 234.
13. Abbott, vol. I, p. 232.
14. Abbott, vol. I, p. 251.
15. Abbott, vol. I, p. 259.
16. Abbott, vol. I, p. 260.
17. Abbott, vol. I, p. 272.
18. Abbott, vol. I, p.287.
19. P. Newman, *The Battle of Marston Moor* (Chichester, 1981), p. 103; A. Woolrych, 'Cromwell as a soldier', in Morrill, *Cromwell*, pp. 100–1.
20. Abbott, vol. I, p. 287.
21. Quoted in C.H. Firth, 'The raising of the Ironsides', *Transactions of the Royal Historical Society*, new series, vol. 13, 1899, pp. 61–2. See pp. 113–14, 143, 152 for the important role this biblical story of Moses and the Israelites had on Cromwell's thinking in the 1650s.
22. Abbott, vol. I, p. 278.
23. This is effectively refuted by L. Kaplan, 'The "plot" to depose Charles I in 1644', *Bulletin of the Institute of Historical Research*, **44**, 1971.
24. R. Baillie, *The Letters and Journals of Robert Baillie* (2 vols, 1841), vol. II, p. 229.
25. Many of Cromwell's charges against Manchester (and Manchester's counter-charges) are printed in J. Bruce (ed.), *The Quarrel Between Manchester and Cromwell* (Camden Society, new series, vol. 12, 1875).
26. See note 8 above.
27. Abbott, vol. I, p. 299.
28. Abbott, vol. I, p. 314.
29. Abbott, vol. I, p. 314.
30. Abbott, vol. I, p. 340.
31. Abbott, vol. I, p. 360.
32. Abbott, vol. I, p. 365.
33. Abbott, vol. I, p. 395.
34. Abbott, vol. I, p. 360.
35. Abbott, vol. I, p. 377.
36. Abbott, vol. I, p. 363.
37. Abbott, vol. I, p. 371.
38. Abbott, vol. I, p. 377.
39. Abbott, vol. I, p. 372.

Chapter 3

THE SEARCH FOR SETTLEMENT (1646–49)

In January 1649 Cromwell was an ardent activist among a tiny clique that pushed through the trial and execution of Charles I against the wishes of the majority represented in parliament. Yet he spent most of the preceding two and a half years working assiduously for a post-war settlement, central to which was the return to power of Charles I. His decision to support those determined to get rid of the king came at a very late stage at the end of what he later described as 'that memorable year', 1648. Why did Cromwell remain committed to reaching a settlement with Charles for so long, much longer than others in the army such as his brother-in-law and fellow army officer, Henry Ireton? And why and when did Cromwell eventually decide that he should no longer work for a monarchical settlement, but rather commit himself to what had been unthinkable only a short time before: the trial and execution of the king?

.   .   .

BEFORE THE PUTNEY DEBATES

Until the end of the Putney Debates in the Army Council in November 1647 there is no indication that Cromwell was considering anything other than a monarchical post-war settlement. As has been seen, by the end of the war Cromwell's aim – the 'cause' – had become identified more than ever before with the army: a concern to achieve just material rewards for the soldiers, and liberty of conscience for Protestants in post-war England. But also integral to the 'cause' was a commitment to regular parliaments, and a desire to bring about a parliamentary settlement with the king. When he returned to parliament in the summer of

1646 he soon discovered, as he had in 1644, that his interpretation of the 'cause' was one that not everyone shared, and that parliamentary hostility to the army and to religious liberty was strong. Yet for nearly twelve months Cromwell worked at Westminster trying to prevent a breach between parliament and the army. By the end of May 1647 that proved impossible and Cromwell, as will be seen, had little alternative but to leave London and rejoin the army. What is (on the face of it) extremely surprising is that this dramatic development did not cause him to alter the political tactics he had been following since the end of the war: during the six months from June 1647 until after the Putney Debates, which saw the army's development into a major independent political force, he continued to work with political allies at Westminster as well as in the army to bring about a negotiated settlement between parliament, the army and the king.

Cromwell's service in the army from March 1645 to June 1646 had been a period of relief, distanced as he was from factional conflicts and political intrigues at Westminster. When he returned to parliament he found that the divisions which had emerged during the political quarrels of the winter of 1644–45 had become harder and deeper. This was not, however, immediately apparent. On his return, a majority in parliament united on the terms to be offered to the king as a basis for settlement. The publication of Charles's correspondence, captured at Naseby, which revealed the king's treacherous negotiations with the Irish and other foreign powers, exchanging promises of favour for Catholicism in return for armed support against the English parliament, appalled many at Westminster and provoked them into agreeing in June to a package of stiff measures – the Propositions of Newcastle – to be sent to the king. In the following weeks, however, it became apparent that this unity was very superficial and that there were, in reality, huge divisions among English parliamentarians. In one sense the contemporary terms used to describe these differences – 'Presbyterians' and 'Independents' – are misleading, because the most obvious divisive issue was political not religious: 'Political Presbyterians' (like the earl of Essex and Denzil Holles) were willing to accept the return of the king on minimal terms, while 'Political Independents' (a coalition including those Cromwell had allied with during the war) wanted cast-iron limitations imposed on Charles before the army should be disbanded and the king allowed to be returned to power. As has often been pointed out, religious divisions sometimes cut across these political alignments: not all Political Presbyterians and Political Independents were, respectively, religious Presbyterians and religious Independents. Yet the ferocity of post-war parliamentary political controversies is inexplicable without taking account of the hopes and fears that many had about the future religious settlement. While not all Political Independents shared Cromwell's and Saye and Sele's commitment to religious Independency, many (like Oliver St John) were in favour of some measure of religious toleration. When Cromwell was in London in September 1644 he had made a brief appearance in the Commons, collaborating with Oliver St John in an effort to modify the religious intolerance of their opponents. They pressed a motion that, when a national Church was re-established, ways should be found to tolerate those with 'tender consciences who cannot in all things submit to the common rule which shall be established'.[1] On the other hand, as time went on, more and more Political Presbyterians, though not doctrinal religious Presbyterians, supported a Presbyterian Church settlement, if only because of the need to cultivate the support of the Scots, who had fought the war principally to export Presbyterianism to England, and of powerful men in the City, who were strongly in favour of establishing a national Presbyterian Church as a means of imposing social order and preventing a dreaded slide into religious licence and anarchy.

During the post-war months, despite the death of Essex in September 1646, the Political Presbyterians came to gain the political initiative at Westminster, especially since their campaign for a speedy settlement and the imposition of religious uniformity was strengthened by petitions from all parts of the country for the abolition of county committees, the end of high taxes and the demobilisation of the army. What is striking is the way in which the army came to be the target of both religious and political criticism. Political Presbyterians saw its demobilisation (leaving only a smaller force for service in Ireland and the creation of a safe, alternative army, purged of Independents and based on the London trained bands) as a means of facilitating a speedy settlement with the king, while religious Presbyterians wanted to get rid of the army because they were convinced it was the seedbed of religious sectarianism and a threat to the existing social order. One of Cromwell's consistent aims in parliament in the first six months of peace was, therefore, to try to protect the army against this double attack. On 14 July he made a long speech in vindication of the army in the Commons, as evidence accumulated that the Political Presbyterians were aiming their campaign specifically at the New Model Army rather than the parliamentary armies in the North and West. On 10 August Cromwell wrote darkly to Fairfax of the 'faction and worse' which characterised the English parliamentary scene.[2] Cromwell was even more specific after a City petition to both houses of parliament on 19 December demanded the disbandment of the New Model Army because it harboured heretics and the imposition of the Presbyterian covenant on all who served parliament: 'how it strikes at the army . . . you will see by the contents of it', he wrote to Fairfax on 21 December.[3] After the departure of the Scots from England in February 1647 there could no longer be any doubt about the way the Political Presbyterians had targeted the New Model Army for special, hostile treatment. As they gained a firm grip on the key parliamentary Derby House Committee, they pushed through parliament in February and March 1647 measures to reduce the New Model Army in size without satisfying its demands for payment of wage arrears or for indemnity against prosecution for actions committed during the war. What is more, proposals were drafted to send the rump of the army to Ireland with Presbyterian officers. Cromwell's letters became gloomier and gloomier, especially since the emphasis on purging the army of Independents was an implicit threat to his own position. On about 11 March 1647 he wrote again to Fairfax: 'there wants not in all the places men who have so much malice against the army as besots them. . . . Never were the spirits of men more embittered than now'.[4] It may have been now that Cromwell complained to Edmund Ludlow that 'it was a miserable thing to serve a Parliament, to whom let a man be never so faithful, if one pragmatical fellow amongst them rise up and asperse him, he shall never wipe it off. Whereas, when one serves under a General, he may do as much service and yet be free from all blame and envy.'[5] As at other times Cromwell's gloom coincided with a serious illness; from 'an impostume' of the head this time, said one source.[6]

It would be a mistake, though, now, and on later occasions when Cromwell faced even more serious crises, to assume that mental depression and physical illness caused him to cease to work and hope for a parliamentary settlement. His political opponents did not carry all before them in parliament: in October 1646 the Political Presbyterians only succeeded in disbanding Massey's army in the West and not the New Model Army; and, probably more personally satisfying for Cromwell, an ordinance was passed conferring on him estates confiscated from the marquis of Winchester worth £2,500 a year, and his wife and family moved from Ely to London to join him. Moreover, at this time even his gloomiest letters are tinged with hope that God would help him and his allies overcome their problems. 'This is our comfort, God is in heaven . . . His and only His Counsel shall stand', he wrote on 21 December 1646;[7] 'the naked simplicity of Christ . . . will overcome all this', he concluded on 11 March 1647.[8] Even his illness was seen as a sign of God's favour: 'it hath pleased God', he wrote on 7 March, 'to raise me out of a dangerous sickness . . . I received in myself the sentence of death, that I might learn to trust in him'.[9] There is no reason to give credence to an unsupported rumour that Cromwell was considering leaving England in the spring to serve in the army of the Elector Palatine in Germany. He was still hopeful that he could prevent a split occurring between parliament and army. Even a Commons' declaration on 29 April that condemned the supporters of an army petition calling for redress of their material grievances as 'enemies of the state and disturbers of the peace' did not change his view. When Cromwell went to the headquarters of the New Model Army at Saffron Walden on 2 May, under parliamentary orders with three other officer MPs, Philip Skippon, Henry Ireton and Charles Fleetwood, he went both to assure the army that a parliamentary ordinance providing legal indemnity for soldiers was under consideration and to persuade the soldiers to remain obedient to parliament. Addressing a meeting of officers in Saffron Walden on 16 May, Cromwell underlined his continuing commitment to a parliamentary settlement. He urged the officers to go back to their regiments and 'work in them a good opinion of that authority [parliament] that is over both us and them. If that authority fall to nothing, nothing can follow but confusion.'[10]

However, what Cromwell saw and heard at Saffron Walden during his nineteen-day stay there, from 2 until 19 May 1647, must at least have caused him to doubt whether he could any longer prevent an open rupture between army and parliament, and to revise the view he had expressed on 22 March that 'he knew the army would disband and lay down their arms at their [parliament's] door, whensoever they should command them'.[11] That may have been true of the army when Cromwell had left it ten months before; when he got to Saffron Walden in May, however, he found the army transformed: it was now erupting into revolt. The view that the New Model Army was a political force from its inception in 1645 and that its politicisation was due largely to infiltration of the army by Leveller ideas can now be discounted. The New Model Army began life as an amalgamation of regiments from existing armies (Manchester's, Essex's and Waller's) and, although not insulated from political events outside, until the spring of 1647 there is no evidence that anyone in it advocated that it act as an independent political force. What primarily caused this to happen was the frontal attack made on it by parliament in the first weeks of 1647. Instead of receiving what the victorious army considered its just rewards, wage arrears and assurances of legal indemnity, parliament proceeded to disband it and to condemn its protests as illegal. The result was to bring about a spontaneous process of politicisation from within the army. It is highly unlikely that Cromwell, any more than the Levellers, had a central part in it. He was a spectator of what was happening at Saffron Walden, trying to dampen the growing sense of outrage among the soldiers. The revolt of the New Model Army was unwelcome to him: it was a major blow to his attempt since the end of the war to act as a mediator keeping army and parliament together.

Exactly when Cromwell decided to leave Westminster and join the army revolt is uncertain. What he had seen at Saffron Walden must have made it fairly certain that the Commons' vote on 25 May, four days after he and the other officer MPs reported on the situation to parliament, to disband the New Model Army would provoke a violent reaction, and make his own position as a champion of the army at Westminster untenable. He probably spent the next few days busily looking after his own personal affairs. On 27 May he and Ireton appealed to the Commons' army committee for payment of their wage arrears, and, unlike the rank-and-file soldiers, were successful. Cromwell was paid arrears of £1,976 on 28 May.[12]

The picture of Cromwell at this time frantically looking after his own affairs and protecting himself and his family against possible attacks from vengeful political opponents is probably nearer the truth than someone calmly engineering Cornet Joyce's seizure of the king from his parliamentary guards at Holmby House in Nottinghamshire, which happened on 4 June. It is true that Joyce visited Cromwell in London *en route* from Oxford to Holmby, but it is likely that Joyce came merely to get Cromwell's blessing for his exploit. The main importance of Joyce's visit is that it convinced Cromwell that Fairfax and the officers were in danger of losing control of the army. His political strategy of the last year lay in ruins, and he had little alternative but to leave London, as he did probably on 3 June, arriving at the army headquarters at Newmarket on the following day.

As on other occasions, so now at this crucial point in his career, it is extremely difficult to discover to what extent the image that some people had of him at the time, and which has been adopted by others later, coincides with historical reality. It is, however, fairly certain that the image of Cromwell developed by his Political Presbyterian opponents and by Royalists as the major 'incendiary' fuelling the army revolt is far from the truth. As has been seen, the army revolt, including Joyce's plan to seize the king, began from within the rank and file of the army and came as a surprise to Cromwell. When he reached the army headquarters on 4 June the process of drafting the army's first major political manifesto, *The Solemn Engagement of the Army*, was already well advanced, and the final version owed more to a group of officers, especially Ireton, than to Cromwell. Moreover, when, as a result of *The Solemn Engagement*, representatives ('agitators') of each regiment were admitted to the General Council of the Army, decision-making in the army involved a process of consultation, involving other senior officers and agitators, as well as Cromwell. It would clearly be foolish to play down Cromwell's influence too much. As has been seen, he was now no political lightweight, but a man of considerable reputation both inside and outside the army. But he appears during the next six months to have used what influence he had in the army, contrary to the Presbyterian view of him, to urge restraint, curbing those who favoured extremist tactics, attempting to calm the fears of those outside its ranks that the army was bent on social and political revolution. He also began again the attempt to secure a settlement between the army, parliament and the king.

The key to Cromwell's activities in the heady six months from June 1647 is that, although he had left Westminster, his links with his parliamentary political allies there remained close. As the army marched slowly southwards towards Uxbridge and then fell back on Reading by 4 July, he and his fellow army officers had frequent meetings with parliamentary commissioners, including his Political Independent friends. The result was that, although the army manifestos of June (principally *The Solemn Engagement* of 5 June and *The Representation of the Army* of 14 June), drafted by Ireton, set out a programme of political change aimed at the impeachment of eleven Political Presbyterian MPs and securing regular parliaments and liberty of conscience, great care was also taken to make it clear that the army was aiming at a monarchical settlement. 'We do not see how there can be any peace to the kingdom', declared an army *Remonstrance* on 23 June, 'without a due consideration of provision for the rights, quiet and immunity of His Majesty, his royal family and his late partakers.'[13] Soothing words too were written to calm fears about the army's insistence on religious liberty. Cromwell and the other signatories of a letter on 10 June assured the City of London that by liberty of conscience they did not mean to interrupt 'the settling of the Presbyterian Government. Nor do we seek to open a way to licentious liberty, under the pretence of obtaining ease for tender consciences'.[14] When the army got to Reading early in July, work began in earnest by Cromwell, Ireton and his parliamentary allies to produce a blueprint for a settlement, *The Heads of the Proposals*, that was officially published on 2 August 1647.

There is now abundant evidence that *The Heads of the Proposals* was not merely the work of Ireton, reflecting only the views of himself and his father-in-law. As John Adamson has recently shown, Cromwell worked closely with his political allies at Westminster, notably Oliver St John and a group of powerful peers, the earls of Northumberland and Pembroke, Lord Wharton and Viscount Saye and Sele.[15] Both Wharton and Saye and Sele were at Reading early in July and their collaboration with Cromwell and Ireton (as will be seen) continued throughout the summer and autumn. When *The Heads of the Proposals* were discussed in the army council at Reading in debates on 16 and 17 July, Cromwell's main aim was to forestall the demands of the agitators that they should march on London to impose a settlement by force. They should, he urged, collaborate with those in parliament 'that have been faithful [to the army] from the sitting of the parliament to this very day' and attempt to reach a negotiated settlement: 'whatsoever you get by a treaty, whatsoever comes to be settled upon us in that way, it will be firm and durable, it will be conveyed over to posterity . . . we shall avoid that great objection that will lie against us, that we have got things of the Parliament by force . . . that which you have by force, I look upon it as nothing'.[16] An attempted 'counter-revolution' in London on 26 July, when a mob, apparently with the connivance of the Political Presbyterian leaders, invaded the chamber of the Commons and invited the king to London, forced Cromwell and his fellow officers to order the military occupation of London on 6 August. But this did not alter the determination of Cromwell and his allies to oppose the use of force and secure a settlement with Charles on the basis of *The Heads of the Proposals*. When Major White at the first of a series of weekly meetings of the Army Council (with agitators present) early in September proposed that there was no visible authority in the kingdom but the power and force of the sword, he was expelled from the council without a protest from anyone in the army.

The Heads of the Proposals was the most explicit statement to date of 'the cause' for which Cromwell and his allies stood. Constitutionally it provided for a restoration of the monarchy, as long as the king first agreed to call regular biennial parliaments, sanction rational reform of parliamentary representation so that it was related more accurately than before to regional variations in population and wealth, and accept parliamentary control of the army and navy, and appointment of the great officers of state for ten years. The centrepiece of its religious provisions was the maintenance of a national Church with bishops and the Book of Common Prayer, but all the coercive powers of bishops were to be abolished, as were laws forcing everyone to attend the national Church. Protestants who did not attend parish churches were to be free to worship in their own ways. Finally, *The Heads* proposed that an Act of Oblivion be passed (excepting only a few noted Royalists), extending legal indemnity from prosecution to those who had supported the king, with the aim of encouraging a general acceptance of the settlement.

Although *The Heads of the Proposals* was a much more generous settlement than any yet offered the king (including the Propositions of Newcastle), with the benefit of hindsight it is possible to see that the settlement was doomed. The memoirs of Sir John Berkeley, one of the intermediaries between the king and the army, makes clear that Charles never intended to negotiate seriously on *The Heads*. But this was not yet apparent. The army 'grandees', Fairfax, Cromwell and Ireton, remained in contact with the king, either directly or through Berkeley and his fellow intermediary, John Ashburnham, as the king was moved during July, August and September from Caversham (near the army camp at Reading) to Woburn, Stoke Poges, Windsor and then to Hampton Court. Charles kept his views to himself and he rejected the revised Propositions of Newcastle when they were given to him in September, indicating that he favoured *The Heads of the Proposals*. Moreover, negotiations, rather than the use of force, seemed also to be bringing about results in parliament, as MPs agreed both to settle the wage arrears of the army and maintain a large military establishment of 26,400 men. Cromwell's allies, especially Wharton and Saye and Sele, began to introduce into the House of Lords most of the major provisions of *The Heads of the Proposals* in the form of parliamentary bills, as part of a political strategy to which Cromwell gave his full support. On 13 October 1647, the day Wharton introduced the religious provisions of *The Heads of the Proposals* in the Lords, Cromwell excused himself to Fairfax from attending a court martial at Windsor because of his parliamentary duties: 'I scarce miss the house a day', he wrote, 'where it's very necessary for me to be.'[17] What is more, on 20 October Cromwell was reported to have made a three-hour speech in the Commons in favour of a monarchical settlement.

The major obstacle to the attempt to reach a settlement on the basis of *The Heads of the Proposals* that became apparent at this stage was not Charles's intransigence, but the opposition of John Lilburne and the Levellers, who were intensely suspicious that the negotiations between Cromwell and his allies (whom they disparagingly nicknamed 'the grandees') and the king would result in an unconditional return of the old political and social order. On 5 September Cromwell visited his one-time friend, Lilburne, in the Tower to try to persuade him not to cause disaffection in the army if he were released. He also urged Lilburne to 'avoide the giving of so great distaste to the House of Peeres at a time when it is so much imported to the army to preserve a fair correspondence with them'.[18] Not surprisingly, Lilburne, who since his resignation from the army in 1645 had been involved in major legal battles with the House of Lords, which had resulted in his imprisonment, was unimpressed by Cromwell's appeal, which may account for Cromwell's jaundiced comment in a letter of 14 September to Michael Jones in Dublin that 'a cloud may lie over our actions to them who are not acquainted with the grounds of our transactions'.[19] His fears were realised when five regiments elected new agitators who had close links with the civilian London Levellers and, although shallow-rooted, Leveller infiltration of the army became significant for the first time. The new agitators produced a long indictment of Cromwell and the grandees, *The Case of the Army Truly Stated,* which was presented to Fairfax on 18 October. This was followed just over a week later by a detailed plan for a constitutional and religious settlement,

The Agreement of the People, as an alternative to *The Heads of the Proposals.* Fairfax and Cromwell responded by referring the plan to a meeting of the Army Council at Putney on 28 October.

The subsequent Putney Debates have become renowned, quite rightly, as a dramatic confrontation between those who argued for a seismic shift in the distribution of power in England and their conservative opponents. However, the debates began rather differently, as an attempt by Cromwell to defend the strategy for a settlement he had followed ever since the end of the war and to defuse the recent Leveller attack on it. His main aim at Putney was to maintain the unity of the army behind a settlement programme based on *The Heads of the Proposals,* and his speeches at Putney are peppered with pleas to this effect: 'I shall speak to nothing but that, as before the Lord, I am persuaded in my heart tends to uniting of us', he said when the debates began on 28 October; and (on the next day) 'Let us be doing but let us be united in our doing.'[20] That this was his prime aim at Putney explains why the first day was spent discussing what has often been seen to be the puzzling issue of whether or not the 'engagements' – the manifestos – issued by the army since June were still binding on it. In the face of Leveller and agitator opposition, Cromwell and Ireton consistently argued that the 'engagements' could not be broken. Instead, on 28 October they proposed that a committee be established to search through the army's previous engagements in order to establish exactly what demands and promises had been made in them. The committee was asked to compare these with the proposals made in *The Agreement,* in the hope that this would reveal significant common ground between the army and the Levellers.

Time after time during the course of the debates Cromwell appeared in the role of mediator, displaying the political skills that he had learned since his inept behaviour in the early months of the Long Parliament. He strove to give the appearance of flexibility, defending himself and the grandees against the 'jealousies and apprehensions' that they were

. . . wedded and glued to forms of government, so that

whatsoever we may pretend, it is in vain for you to speak to us. . . . You will find that we are far from being so particularly engaged to anything . . . that we should not concur with you that the foundation and supremacy is in the people, radically in them, and to be set down by them in their representations.[21]

When the divisive issue of the franchise was raised, unlike the uncompromising Ireton, Cromwell suggested that there might be a case for an extension of the vote. 'Perhaps', he said on 29 October, 'there are a very considerable part of copyholders by inheritance that ought to have a voice, and there may be somewhat too reflects upon the generality of the people.'[22]

At times he sought to cool rising tempers by shunting divisive issues into committees, and (on 28 October) by supporting the idea of interrupting the debate by a prayer meeting. 'Perhaps God', he said, 'may unite us and carry us both one way.'[23]

However, this did not happen. On the contrary, as the debates continued disagreement grew rather than diminished. When the committee that had been given the task of analysing the army's engagements met on 29 October, Cromwell and the other officers made 'a great error of judgement'[24] in allowing the agitator representatives to depart from the committee's agenda to discuss the first clause of *The Agreement of the People*, relating to the franchise. Moreover, at a later meeting of the full Army Council on 5 November (when Cromwell may have been absent) the radical representatives pushed through a decision to write a letter to the Commons from the council disowning the army's commitment to continuing negotiations with the king. The decision was overturned a few days later, but by 8 November it was clear that Cromwell's tactic of steering clear of divisive issues had failed, and he announced that the army council debates would end in a week's time with three separate army rendezvous outside London. Although Cromwell's contributions to the remaining debates were only sporadically reported, the fragmentary record suggests that he now came out unequivocally against extending the vote (it tended, he is reported to have said, 'very much to anarchy')[25] and he made clear his continued commitment to a monarchical settlement. The well-known story of Cromwell's leading role in quashing an army mutiny at one of the three rendezvous at Ware, in Hertfordshire, has recently been questioned, despite reports from varied contemporary sources which suggest otherwise.[26] What is certain is that he approved of what was done. He later told Edmund Ludlow that the execution of the mutineers at Ware was 'absolutely necessary to keep things from falling into confusion; which must have ensued upon that division if it had not been timely prevented'.[27] As at other times, as will be seen, Cromwell had no compunction in acting ruthlessly when the unity of the army was threatened.

Did Cromwell also engineer the king's escape from Hampton Court on 11 November, which undoubtedly made easier the task of imposing military discipline? As on other crucial occasions in Cromwell's career, the evidence does not suggest clear-cut conclusions. He *may* have had a hand in the king's escape, but what makes this extremely unlikely is that the escape was bound to be, at the very least, a severe setback to the chances of securing a settlement between the king, parliament and the army, for which Cromwell and his allies had been working for months.

. . .

AFTER THE PUTNEY DEBATES

From the early 1640s Cromwell's political career had been closely connected with the group of civilian MPs and peers, notably Oliver St John and Viscount Saye and Sele. In 1648 Cromwell parted company with his former allies, as he, unlike them, at the end of the year acquiesced in the army's purge of parliament and, then, enthusiastically supported the trial and execution of the king and the establishment of the English republic. This break was of momentous significance in the development of Cromwell's career. It is true that on occasions before 1648 parliamentary opposition to his hopes of securing a measure of religious liberty and a settlement of the army's grievances had caused him to doubt whether his two aims of achieving parliamentary liberties and godly reformation could be reconciled. At the Reading Debates in July 1647, for example, he had raised the dilemma of whether it was better to bring about a settlement by consultation with the 'people' or by force: 'that's the question, what's for the people's good, not what pleases them'.[28] But he had concluded, as has been seen, that a settlement negotiated by parliament was superior. 'I do not know that force is to be used except we cannot get what is for the good of the kingdom without force'. Force was only to be used 'but in a way of necessity'.[29] However, at the end of 1648 – 'that memorable year' – he did countenance the use of force against parliament. As will be seen, he did this with great reluctance: his break with parliament was far from permanent and he subsequently spent much of his political energies trying to return to the ways of constitutional respectability. But what happened in 1648 made that task more difficult than ever. Why did Cromwell (unlike his former allies) commit himself to the use of force and unconstitutional action? Why did a man who hitherto had supported a parliamentary and monarchical settlement disregard the rights and privileges of parliament and execute the king? A useful starting point for answering that question is a phrase Cromwell used in a declaration on 26 December 1648, when he announced his support for bringing the king to trial: 'providence and necessity', he said, 'had cast them [him and his fellow army officers] upon it'.[30]

In the weeks after the end of the Putney Debates 'necessity' – the dictates of political reality – gave Cromwell and his allies little alternative but to break off negotiations with the king. When Charles's emissary, Berkeley, came to the Army Council at Windsor on 28 November he received a very cool reception from officers who mistrusted what he might do after his escape from Hampton Court to the Isle of Wight. This mistrust was confirmed when, in December, Charles rejected the Four Bills, parliament's package of measures as the minimal conditions for further negotiations sent to him before his escape. What damaged Charles's reputation even more seriously was that in December he also allied with a conservative faction in Scotland, led by the duke of Hamilton, making an 'Engagement' promising to establish Scottish Presbyterianism in England for three years in return for Scottish armed support to restore him to power. What made this even more serious is that it coincided with a protest movement in Kent against the army, which was later repeated in similar outbreaks in southern England and south Wales, known as 'the second Civil War'. Therefore at the end of 1647 Cromwell and other army officers began a series of meetings with senior parliamentarians, planning the parliamentary campaign that resulted on 3 January 1648 in the passage of a Vote of No Addresses, declaring that the Commons 'will make no further addresses or applications to the King'. Cromwell made a fervent speech in its support, threatening MPs who hesitated to vote for the motion: 'expose not the honest party of the Kingdom, who have bled for you, and suffer not misery to fall upon them, for want of corage and resolution in you, els the honest party may take such courses as nature dictates them'.[31] A Royalist account gave an extra gloss to Cromwell's militancy; as he spoke, it was said, 'the glow-worm glistening in his beak, he began to spit fire', and he was reported to have concluded his speech by putting his hand on his sword.[32]

For Denzil Holles, a Political Presbyterian leader, the Vote was a watershed: 'the Catastrophe of this Tragedy, the last and most horrid Act' before the execution of the king.[33] But Holles was wrong. Within a few weeks many who had supported the Vote of No Addresses began to breach it, and even Cromwell's Political Independent allies resumed tentative negotiations with the king on the Isle of Wight. It may be that, like them, Cromwell felt that, despite Charles's activities in December, it might still be possible to detach him from a Scottish alliance before the expected invasion of England took place. There is, though, nothing to support a Royalist rumour in April that Cromwell visited the king on the Isle of Wight.[34] Not for the first or last time Cromwell was very successful in covering his tracks. In the first months of 1648 his few recorded statements are as puzzling to historians as they must have been to contemporaries. Edmund Ludlow recorded a meeting at Cromwell's house in King Street, Westminster, early in the year, when some 'Commonwealthsmen', including Ludlow, raised the possibility of a republican settlement, at which Cromwell and his 'grandee' friends 'kept themselves in the clouds, and would not declare their judgements either for a monarchical, aristocratical or democratical government; maintaining that any of them might be good in themselves, or for us, according as providence should direct'. When pressed to give his views further by Ludlow, Cromwell 'took up a cushion and flung it at my [Ludlow's] head, and then ran down the stairs'. Next day Ludlow met Cromwell in the Commons and pressed him again on the question of a republic, to which he got a reply that is a masterpiece of equivocation: 'he was convinced of the desirableness of what was proposed', Cromwell said, 'but not the feasibleness of it'.[35] Equally frustrating as this ambiguous evidence is the fact that in the first months of 1648 it is not even known where Cromwell was on crucial occasions. The most glaring gap in our knowledge of him at this time is his whereabouts on 28 April 1648. There is no certain evidence that he was even in the House of Commons on that day, when a vote was passed formally breaching the Vote of No Addresses, in favour of a motion not to 'alter the fundamental government of the kingdom, by King, Lords and Commons', let alone that he voted for it, as did Political Independents like Henry Vane junior and William Pierrepoint. Nor is it known whether or not he was, on the same day, at a meeting of the Army Council at Windsor, which the officers spent in prayer, seeking the Lord's guidance. All that is certain about Cromwell's attitude until this point is that he had not committed himself openly (like his Political Independent allies) to revoking the Vote of No Addresses, nor to using force against parliament and the king.

What converted Cromwell to the use of force against parliament and to regicide were his experiences during the second Civil War, which he interpreted as signs that providence had selected him and the army for that purpose. This was no sudden overnight conversion, but during the period he was away from London, from the end of April until after his return to London on 6 December 1648, he gradually came to see events in a totally different light from those who did not take part in the war, including his Political Independent allies, who were supporting negotiations with the king at Newport on the Isle of Wight. Unlike them, 'providence' as well as 'necessity' drove Cromwell towards revolution.

In some ways, the effects of the second Civil War on Cromwell were very similar to those of the first war. As in 1645 Cromwell found life with his military companions a refreshing change from the hard political dilemmas he faced at Westminster. As he set out from Windsor at the end of April 1648 to put down a rebellion in South Wales he no longer had to weigh his words carefully as he had in the dangerous political world of Westminster. He was now able to make bold, dynamic speeches, reaffirming his brotherhood with fellow soldiers, based on the common experiences of the first war. On 8 May, speaking at the head of each of his regiments at Gloucester, he reminded his soldiers how 'he had often times ventured his life with them and they with him, against the common enemy of the kingdom . . . [he] desired them to arm themselves with the same resolution as formerly . . . and that for his part, he protested to live and die with them'.[36] In a letter to a captain of the Gloucestershire militia on the following day he urged support for 'the Parliament's cause',[37] and this and other letters at this time vibrate with the same decisive urgency seen in those written in 1643, when the Eastern Association faced the threat of being overrun by the earl of Newcastle's army. After the intrigues of the past few months Cromwell enjoyed being a man of action once more, dealing again with practical matters. He made sure his army was supplied with the right size of shells: 'the depth of them we desire may be fourteen inches and three-quarters of an inch', he wrote to the committee at Carmarthen on 9 June.[38] After the resistance in South Wales had been broken by the surrender of the rebels' leaders, Laugharne and Poyer, at Pembroke on 11 July, he turned to the North to meet the invading Scottish army, stopping at Northampton and Coventry to pick up supplies of shoes and stockings for his troops.

As in the first Civil War, Cromwell's military reputation was greatly enhanced. His rapid march northwards to rendezvous with Major-General John Lambert, the commander of the English army in the North, and his victory over the Scottish army at Preston on 17 August has been hailed recently as displaying 'generalship of a high order'.[39] Moreover, as in the early 1640s, this and other victories that helped bring an end to the second Civil war brought another rush of confidence that God was with him. As after Marston Moor and Naseby, his letters after Preston resound with elation at the 'unspeakable mercy' of the victory and the certainty that it had been brought about by 'the great hand of God'.[40]

In one major respect, however, the second Civil War affected Cromwell in a way that the first had not. Just before he left for South Wales, he attended the second day of the Army Council's prayer meeting at Windsor on 29 April, when he was reported to have urged his brother officers 'to a thorough consideration of our actions as an army, as well as ways particularly as private Christians, to see if any iniquity could be found in them, and what it was, that if possible we might find it out and so remove the cause of such sad rebukes which were upon us by reason of our iniquities'.[41]

During the second Civil War Cromwell became convinced that he had found the major cause of 'such sad rebukes' in the leniency shown to the 'contrivers and authors' of renewed war. The second Civil War was, he believed, 'a more prodigious Treason than any that had been perpetrated before, because the former quarrel . . . was that Englishmen might rule over one another; this [is] to vassalise us to a foreign nation'.[42] Significantly Cromwell reviled the Scottish Engagers who had allied with the king for their resistance to the English, despite 'the witness that God had borne against your army in the invasion of this kingdom'; while those Scotsmen who had opposed the Engagers and who he helped to put into power in Scotland after his victory at Preston were praised by him as 'Christians and men of honour'.[43] But his anger was directed mainly against those in England who had opposed the army in 1648. 'Their fault who have appeared in this summer's business is certainly double to theirs who were in the first, because it is the repetition of the same offence against all the witnesses that God has borne, by making and abetting to a second war.'[44] After the defeat of the Welsh rebels he called for vengeance on their leaders, Laugharne and Poyer: their 'iniquity', he said, was 'double, because they have sinned against so much light, and against so many evidences of Divine Presence going along with and prospering a righteous cause, in the management of which they had a share'.[45] They (like Colonel Humphrey Matthews) had been parliamentarians in the first war, and, when Matthews was only fined for his offence in September, Cromwell was full of 'amazement . . . to see such manifest witness-ings of God (so terrible and so just) no more rev-erenced'.[46]

Cromwell was not alone in the army in calling for divine vengeance on their enemies. After the defeat of the Essex and Kent rebels at the siege of Colchester in August Fairfax executed two of the leaders of the rebellion after a sum-mary court martial. More importantly, on 18 November Ire-ton persuaded the Army Council at St Albans to accept a *Remonstrance* which called for a purge of parliament and the king's trial. One of the arguments for this was that the king's defeat in the second Civil War was a sign by God that Charles Stuart, 'the capital and grand author of all our troubles', should be brought to justice.[47] However, dra-matic as had been the effects on Cromwell of the second Civil War, he was not yet prepared to go as far as that. As at the beginning of the army revolt in 1647, so now at the climax of it at the end of 1648, Cromwell was not a central participant. During November he remained in the North, at Pontefract, where a few opponents of the army still held out. Many of his letters in November are as puzzlingly am-biguous as any he wrote. There are signs in them that using force against parliament was very much in his mind: on 6 November he reminded his friend Robin Hammond that there was a precedent for this in recent events in Scot-land where 'a lesser party of a Parliament hath made it lawful to declare the greater part a faction, and made the Parliament null, and call a new one, and to do this by force . . . . Think of the example and of the conse-quence.'[48] A few days later he attended a meeting of repre-sentatives of northern regiments at York, which drafted petitions in support of the regiments with Fairfax and Ire-ton in the South. Cromwell sent these petitions to Fairfax, telling of his officers 'very great zeal to have impartial jus-tice done upon Offenders, and I must confess, I do in all, from my heart, concur with them . . . they are things which God puts into our hearts'.[49] But when Fairfax com-manded him to come south on 28 November (an order he probably received two days later) it was six days before he reached London, and he did not arrive until after Ireton had expelled from parliament about a hundred MPs con-sidered to be opponents of the army.

Was Cromwell's delay in committing himself to the revolutionary methods being followed by his son-in-law due to political guile, or was he still genuinely undecided about what to do next and (as he said) 'in a waiting posture, desiring to see what the Lord would lead us to'?[50] It would be foolish to disregard his ability to act with great political cunning – he was now no longer the political innocent he had been before 1642, and which he still sometimes portrayed himself as being. Yet it is possible that his delay in coming south at this time was, in part at least, motivated by the hope that (if he was not too closely associated with the radical rhetoric of the army) he might still be able to work with his Political Independent allies to secure Charles's agreement to some kind of settlement, perhaps one with the duke of Gloucester, Charles's second son, as king. After Cromwell reached London he rarely attended meetings of the Army Council, where Ireton pushed ahead with arangements for the king's trial. Instead, although Cromwell lived in Whitehall and 'lay in one of the king's rich beds', he had frequent meetings with the lawyers, Bulstrode Whitelocke and Thomas Widdrington, 'to consider and confer how the settlement of the kingdom might be best effected' by securing an agreement with the king, using the earl of Denbigh as an intermediary.[51] These negotiations collapsed on about 26 December 1648, when Whitelocke hastily left London for the safety of his house in Henley in Oxfordshire. It was only at this stage that Cromwell at last joined Ireton's revolution and enthusiastically committed himself to the trial of the king.

Many of Cromwell's actions during the next few weeks, which saw the trial and execution of the king, the abolition of monarchy and the House of Lords, and the establishment of the English Republic are seen through the distorting evidence of witnesses in treason trials in 1660 who were desperately trying to steer the blame for what had happened away from themselves and onto Cromwell. It therefore needs to be emphasised that Cromwell was not the only leader of the English Revolution, but was one among a small group of men who together pushed it through. Yet later reports perhaps do accurately reflect his impulsive and decisive support for it, once he had thrown off the indecision of the previous weeks. 'I tell you [Algernon Sydney wrote in 1660, reporting Cromwell's reactions to his own legal objections to bringing the king to trial] 'we will cut off his [the king's] head with the crown on it.'[52] What drove Cromwell to take this drastic step was 'necessity'. It was now patently clear to all that it was impossible to secure an agreement with a king who had no intention of concluding one. But what also precipitated him to take violent action was his conviction that Charles I was not just a war criminal who had plunged the country into renewed Civil War, but that he was a sinful man whose death was required by God in order to gain God's blessing. When Thomas Brook printed a sermon he delivered to the House of Commons on 27 December 1648, he attached to it a text from the Old Testament book of Numbers (35.33): 'Ye shall not pollute the Land wherin yee are; for bloud, it defileth the Land, and the Land cannot be cleansed of the bloud that is shed therin, but by the bloud of him that shed it.'[53] This was a sentiment shared by Cromwell. In January 1650 he wrote to his old Political Independent friend, Lord Wharton, defending what he had done a year previously: 'Be not offended at the manner; perhaps no other way was left'. To underline the point, like Thomas Brook, he referred specifically to a story in the book of Numbers: the case of Phineas, who had executed summary justice by thrusting a javelin through the bellies of a sinful copulating couple, so saving Israel from God's wrath through an outbreak of plague. The case of the execution of Charles Stuart was very similar, Cromwell argued, and God approved of it: 'God accepted the zeal [when] reason might have called for a jury.'[54] Just as religious enthusiasm politicised Cromwell in the 1630s, so it also drove him to execute the king in 1649.

.   .   .

NOTES AND REFERENCES

1. S.R. Gardiner, *History of the Great Civil War* (reprint edn, Windrush Press, 1987, 4 vols), vol. II, p. 30.
2. Abbott, vol. I, p. 410.
3. Abbott, vol. I, p. 420.
4. Abbott, vol. I, p. 430.
5. C.H. Firth (ed.), *Memoirs of Edmund Ludlow* (Clarendon Press, 2 vols, 1894), vol. I, pp. 144–5.

6. Abbott, vol. I, p. 426.
7. Abbott, vol. I, p. 421.
8. Abbott, vol. I, p. 430.
9. Abbott, vol. I, pp. 428–9.
10. *Clarke Papers,* vol. I, p. 72.
11. Abbott, vol. I, p. 433.
12. C. Hoover, 'Cromwell's status and pay in 1646–7', *Historical Journal,* **23**, 1980, p. 708.
13. Quoted in A. Woolrych, *Soldiers and Statesmen: the General Council of the Army and its Debates, 1647–8* (Clarendon Press, 1987), p. 142.
14. Abbott, vol. I, p. 460.
15. J.S.A. Adamson, 'The English nobility and the projected settlement of 1647', *Historical Journal,* **30**, 1987.
16. Abbott, vol. I, pp. 481–3.
17. Abbott, vol. I, p. 510.
18. Quoted in Adamson, 'The English nobility', p. 595.
19. Abbott, vol. I, p. 506.
20. Abbott, vol. I, pp. 519, 530.
21. Abbott, vol. I, pp. 527–8.
22. Abbott, vol. I, p. 533.
23. Abbott, vol. I, p. 524.
24. J.S. Morrill, 'The army revolt of 1647', in C.A. Tamse and A.C. Duke (eds), *Britain and the Netherlands* (1987), p. 72.
25. Abbott, vol. I, p. 549.
26. M.A. Kishlansky, 'What happened at Ware?', *Historical Journal,* vol. 25, 1982 denies that Cromwell was there. The evidence presented in Woolrych, *Soldiers and Statesmen,* pp. 281–4 has persuaded me that Cromwell was present at Ware.
27. Ludlow, *Memoirs,* vol. I, p. 246.
28. Abbott, vol. I, p. 486.
29. Abbott, vol. I, pp. 483, 478.
30. Abbott, vol. I, p. 719.
31. D. Underdown, 'The parliamentary diary of John Boys 1647–48', *Bulletin of the Institute of Historical Research,* **39**, 1966, p. 156.
32. Abbott, vol. I, p. 576.
33. *Memoirs of Denzil Holles* in F. Maseres (ed), *Select Tracts Relating to the Civil Wars in England* (1815), p. 303.
34. J. Adamson, 'Oliver Cromwell and the Long Parlia-

ment' in Morrill, *Cromwell*, p. 78 does not share my doubts about the untrustworthiness of these reports.

35. Ludlow, *Memoirs*, vol. I, pp. 184–86.
36. Abbott, vol. I, p. 606.
37. Abbott, vol. I, p. 607.
38. Abbott, vol. I, p. 611.
39. A. Woolrych, 'Cromwell as a soldier' in Morrill, *Cromwell*, p. 110.
40. Abbott, vol. I, pp. 633, 638.
41. Abbott, vol. I, pp. 598–9.
42. Abbott, vol. I, p. 691.
43. Abbott, vol. I, p. 661.
44. Abbott, vol. I, p. 691.
45. Abbott, vol. I, p. 621.
46. Abbott, vol. I, p. 692.
47. J.P. Kenyon, (ed.), *The Stuart Constitution: Documents and Commentary* (Cambridge University Press, 2nd ed., 1986), p. 288.
48. Abbott, vol. I, p. 678.
49. Abbot, vol. I, p. 690.
50. Abbott, vol. I, p. 698.
51. B. Whitelocke (ed.), *Memorials of the English Affairs* (Oxford University Press, 4 vols, 1853), vol. II, p. 477.
52. Abbott, vol. I, p. 736.
53. R. Jeffs (ed.), *The English Revolution: Fast Sermons to Parliament, vol. 32, 1648–49* (Cornmarket Press, 1971), p. 81.
54. Abbott, vol. II, pp. 189–90.

Chapter 4

CROMWELL AND THE RUMP (1649–53)

Among the many things that makes Cromwell such an interesting figure is that his character embraced two divergent trends that had emerged in England in the 1640s: the radical desire of a minority for godly reformation, and the conservative yearning of the majority of the political nation for a return to the traditional ways of government by monarchs who ruled in co-operation with their greater subjects and who called regular parliaments. During the second Civil War Cromwell had come face to face with the fact that at that time it was impossible to reconcile these two aims. If 'the parliamentary cause' had triumphed in 1648 a treaty would have been concluded with the king at Newport on the Isle of Wight, which would have allowed him to return with only minimal limitations placed on his power, and the measure of religious freedom so far gained would have been ousted by the restoration of an intolerant, autocratic national Church. What made 1648 such a traumatic, if 'memorable year', for Cromwell is that he had had to choose between the two 'causes' for which he had striven since 1640, and reluctantly he had sacrificed the parliamentary cause for the godly cause. One result was that from now on the task of reconciling these two causes became harder than ever. The godly cause became more than ever identified with the army, which had arbitrarily purged parliament and executed the king, and to the ranks of outraged parliamentary opinion was now added the formidable group of Political Independents, who had broken with Cromwell.

Nevertheless, very soon after the king's execution Cromwell, before he left London with the army on expeditions to defend the infant republic against its enemies in Ireland and Scotland, began trying to reconcile the parliamentary classes to what had happened as his desire for constitutional respectability reasserted itself. Yet his commitment to godly reformation remained strong. Indeed, during the campaigns in Ireland and Scotland, Cromwell became clearer in his own mind about what he intended the godly reformation of England to entail, and he returned from the battlefield, after the defeat of the king's army at Worcester in September 1651, more determined than ever to bring it about. His disillusionment at his and the army's failure to persuade the Rump Parliament to co-operate during the next two years was, therefore, very great, provoking him in April 1653 impulsively to use force again. In April 1653 he forcibly dissolved the Rump Parliament, explaining (as he had done in 1648–49) that he had 'been led by necessity and providence, to act as we have done'.[1]

. . .

BEFORE WORCESTER

Ironically, one of the reasons why the Rump Parliament did not fill the radical role of heir to the English Revolution of 1648–49 expected of it by Cromwell and his friends in the army and the religious sects can be found in his success immediately after the execution of the king in persuading men of conservative views to support the new regime. The key to many of his activities in the months immediately after the Revolution, before he went to Ireland in August, is his statement to army officers on 23 March 1649 depicting himself as

> . . . a poor man that desires to see the work of God to prosper in our hands, I think there is more cause of danger from division amongst ourselves than by any thing from our enemies . . . [but] if we do not depart from God, and disunite by that departure, and fall into disunion amongst ourselves, I am confident, we doing our duty and waiting upon the Lord, we shall find He will be as a wall of brass round about us till we have finished that work that He has for us to do.[2]

With unity in mind he seems to have made a major effort early in 1649 to persuade those parliamentarians who were horrified at the use of force to accept what had happened in December 1648 and January 1649. On the day after the king's execution, John Owen (Cromwell's religious confidant, who was to be appointed army chaplain to the Irish expeditionary force in July) urged the Commons to woo 'fainters in difficult seasons [and] Labour to recover others, even all that were ever distinguished and called by the name of the Lord, from their late fearful returning to sinful compliance with the enemies of God and the nation'. Shortly afterwards Owen delivered a sermon urging reconciliation between Presbyterians and Independents, and, if Cromwell did not encourage Owen to make such remarks he certainly agreed with them. On 12 April Cromwell spoke in the Commons asking that MPs still excluded after Pride's Purge be allowed to return to their seats and that 'the presbyterian [Church] government may be settled, promising his endeavours thereto'.[3]

Cromwell also made a special effort to rebuild political bridges with his long-time Political Independent allies. He may have persuaded Bulstrode Whitelocke and Henry Vane junior to return to the Commons in the weeks immediately after the Revolution; and his unsuccessful attempt to prevent the abolition of the House of Lords in the Commons on 6 February was probably made to woo his aristocratic ex-allies. The Commons were 'mad, to take these courses to incense the Peers against them, at such a time when they had more need to study a near union with them', said Cromwell, echoing what he had said to Lilburne in September 1647, when he and his aristocratic allies were pushing hard to secure agreement on *The Heads of the Proposals*.[4] Cromwell, too was instrumental in securing the appointment to the new Council of State of some of his friends, such as Sir William Masham, Sir William Armyn and Sir Gilbert Pickering, who had opposed Pride's Purge and the king's execution. When twenty-two of the forty-one members nominated to the new Council refused to take an oath specifically approving the purge and execution, Cromwell moved on 22 February in the Commons that a compromise version of the oath be accepted with the offending words removed. Councillors were, in the Cromwellian version, merely required to swear adherence 'to the present parliament in the maintenance and defence of the publique libertie of the nation as it is now declared by this parliament . . . and in the maintenance and defence of their resolutions concerning the settling of the government of the nation for future in the way of a republique'.[5] Two days later Whitelocke had supper with Cromwell, who was 'very chearful and seemed extremely well pleased', perhaps at the way he had managed to clear the way for the return of some secluded MPs and for the establishment of the Council of State.[6]

Consistent with Cromwell's attempt to secure conservative support for the new regime was the hard line he took at this time against Lilburne and the Levellers, who during the previous weeks had been wooed by the representatives of the army and parliament in discussions at Whitehall, ensuring Leveller quiescence during the critical period as the army occupied London.[7] However, this was only a temporary alliance, and by February Lilburne was thoroughly disenchanted with the new regime. In February and March he published in two parts *England's New Chains Discovered*, a swingeing indictment of the regime, for which he was arrested and taken before the Council of State. Lilburne's account of what he heard Cromwell say to his fellow councillors after he had been taken from the room comes, of course, from a suspect source, but it rings true: 'I tell you, sir, you have no other way to deal with these men but to break them or they will break you', Cromwell is alleged to have said. 'I tell you again, you are meant to break them.'[8] This iron fist of Cromwell can be seen, too, in the way in which he restored discipline in the army, when mutinies broke out in the Spring in London, Banbury and Salisbury. In May he rode before army regiments in Hyde Park and Andover (Hampshire) promising, as at Saffron Walden two years earlier, 'parliament's great care and pains for the army', and appealing for them to 'unite and with unanimous spirit follow him for the subduing of the army revolters which are now called by the name of Levellers'.[9] Then Cromwell and Fairfax in a rapid overnight march from Hampshire to Oxfordshire caught up with the Salisbury mutineers at Burford, where on 14 May one of the ringleaders was shot. It was Cromwell's aim to attract conservative support for the new republic and his efforts to bring under control the 'wild men' in and outside the army were designed, in part, to do that. Like leaders of other regimes in the past and in more recent times, Cromwell also saw the advantage of using campaigns against foreign threats to English security as a means of courting popularity at home. The prospect of being 'subject to the kingdom of Scotland and the kingdom of Ireland, for the bringing in of the king', he thought, might frighten into supporting the infant republic even those who were in favour of a treaty with the king. 'That should awaken all Englishmen', he said in March 1649, 'who perhaps are willing enough he [Charles II] should have come in upon an accommodation, but not that he must come from Ireland and Scotland.'[10]

In the period before he went to Ireland Cromwell's conservatism is much more apparent than his commitment to reformation, raising the possibility that had he stayed at Westminster he might have been seduced by the Rump's drift towards conservatism and have abandoned hopes of reformation. The major importance of his last experience of war between August 1649 and September 1651 in Ireland and Scotland is that it took him away from these temptations and subjected him again to the radical demands of God and the army. On 15 March Cromwell was named as commander of the Irish expedition. For two weeks he hesitated before accepting the post and he delayed departing for Ireland with the expeditionary force until August, when he was certain that his army was well-supplied. His delay was not caused by any doubts about the necessity of fighting the Irish. 'If nothing were done', he said in March,

> . . . we shall not only have . . . our interest rooted out there, but they will in a very short time be able to land forces in England and to put us to trouble here . . . I had rather be overrun with a Cavalierish interest than a Scotch interest; I had rather be overrun with a Scotch interest than an Irish interest; and I think of all this is most dangerous. If they shall be able to carry on their work, they will make this the most miserable people in the earth, for all the world knows their barbarism – not of any religion, almost any of them, but in a manner as bad as Papists.[11]

As will be seen, Cromwell's attitude to the Scottish opponents of the English republic was much less hostile, and fighting them troubled his conscience. He had no such problems when he went to Ireland. Cromwell had an image of the Irish, held by many Protestant Englishmen, and during the 1640s his view of the Irish Rebellion of 1641 as a Catholic massacre of innocent Protestants did not change. In March 1647 he offered £1,000 of the £2,500 granted him by parliament to support the war against the Irish, and his letters and speeches during the rest of his life reflect the belief that many had of the 'crimes' committed by Irish Catholics in 1641, transforming a peaceful and prosperous country into 'a bleeding nation', as he said in a speech on his arrival in Dublin on 15 August.[12] His most forthright views of the Irish were published in a Declaration to the Irish Catholic clergy in January 1650:

> You, unprovoked, put the English to the most unheard of and most barbarous massacre (without respect of sex or age) that ever the sun beheld. And at a time when Ireland was in perfect peace . . . . You are a part of Antichrist, whose Kingdom the Scriptures so expressly speaks should be laid in blood . . . and ere it be long, you must all of you have blood to drink; even the dregs of the cup of the fury and wrath of God, which will be poured out unto you.[13]

It is not surprising that Cromwell's conduct of the war is the most significant difference between his Irish and Scottish campaigns. The brutal behaviour of his troops towards soldiers and civilians alike – for which he was personally responsible – at the first engagement of the war, the siege of Drogheda (3–10 September 1649), and that he sanctioned at the siege of Wexford (2–10 October 1649), was not extraordinary in the context of the punitive treatment meted out to civilians by European armies in the Thirty Years' War and by other commanders in Ireland. But Cromwell had never before initiated or approved massacres like those committed by his troops at Drogheda and Wexford. At Wexford alone at least 2,000 people, including civilians, were killed. As has been seen, Cromwell singled out the leaders of the opposition to the army in England and Wales in 1648 as war criminals, but in Ireland he seems to have considered *all* opponents of the English republic (including civilians and English Protestant allies of the Irish, as well as Irish Catholic soldiers) as being implicated in the 'crimes' of 1641. At Drogheda the governor, Sir Arthur Aston, was an Englishman (Aston had been Royalist governor of Reading at Oxford during the first Civil War) and most of the garrison were English, but their deaths and those of the inhabitants of the town were seen by Cromwell as 'a righteous judgment of God upon those barbrous wretches, who have imbrued their hands in so much innocent blood'.[14] The massacre and plunder committed by his troops after the capture of Wexford, he considered took place because, although he had not ordered it,

> God would not have it so; but by an unexpected providence, in His righteous justice, brought a just judgment upon them, causing them to become a prey to the soldier, who in their piracies had made preys of so many families, and made with their bloods to answer the cruelties which they had exercised upon the lives of divers poor Protestants.[15]

Revenge was not Cromwell's only motive for the brutality he condoned at Wexford and Drogheda, but it was the dominant one, as it was not when he went to Scotland in June 1650.

There are, however, similarities between Cromwell's experiences in Ireland and Scotland. In both countries, although his military record was not an unqualified success, he did win major victories, making the infant republic safe from external threats, and he emerged from the wars with his military reputation higher than ever. The effects on Cromwell the politician were equally dramatic. The image he gained as military saviour of the republic gave him a greater capacity to influence affairs in England than ever before, and his victories gave him the confidence to press for reformation in England, countering the conservative instincts that had revived in the wake of the king's execution to follow the route of constitutional moderation and settlement.

After the capture of Drogheda and Wexford Cromwell's troops did not carry all before them. A subsidiary justification Cromwell gave for 'the bitterness' at Drogheda is one used for the bombing of Hiroshima in 1945 and after, that 'it will tend to prevent the effusion of blood for the future' by striking terror into other garrisons, forcing them to surrender without a struggle.[16] This did not always happen. As the Cromwellian army marched south from Dublin after the capture of Drogheda and Wexford the garrisons at Duncannon and Waterford successfully held out in November and December. His army was ravaged by dysentry: 'our foot falling sick near ten of a company every night', he wrote on 19 December, and he too was 'crazy in his health'.[17] Later, in the the spring, on 27 April 1650, about 2,000 Cromwellian troops were killed attempting to take Clonmel in south-west Ireland. Ireton called that disaster 'the heaviest we ever endured, either in England or here'.[18] Despite these setbacks, when Cromwell left Ireland in May 1650 he had broken the back of Irish resistance. This was not, however, entirely due to his own efforts. There were other considerations, for instance Colonel Michael Jones's victory at Rathmines on 2 August 1649, before Cromwell arrived in Ireland, ensured that the Royalist commander in Ireland, James Butler earl of Ormonde, was never able again to put an army in the field and instead had to rely on guerrilla warfare and garrisoning towns rather than pitched battles, to oppose Cromwell. There was also the work of Cromwell's subordinates, especially that of Robert Boyle, Lord Broghill, younger son of the earl of Cork, whose Anglo-Irish Protestant ancestry made him well-placed to convert many Protestant Royalists in south-west Ireland to the Cromwellian cause in the winter of 1649–50. Above all, the fatal divisions among Cromwell's opponents in Ireland probably went a long way towards ensuring their defeat. Nevertheless it was Cromwell who got a hero's reception when he returned to England in ceremonies on Hounslow Heath and in Hyde Park on 1 June 1650 and when he received a formal vote of thanks from the Commons on 4 June. 'And now the Irish are asham'd', wrote Marvell in a literary tribute,

To see themselves in one Year tam'd
So much one Man can do,
That does both act and know.
They can affirm his Praises best,
And have, though overcome, confest

How good he is, how just,
And fit for highest Trust:
Nor yet grown stiffer with Command,
But still in the Republick's hand:
How fit he is to sway
That can so well obey[19]

The effect of Cromwell's Irish experiences was not con-
fined to enhancing the legends of his military invincibility
and as a saviour of the republic. What he had seen had a
major effect on his political development. He returned
from Ireland more than ever aware of the kind of godly
society he wanted to achieve in England. He considered
that 'the whole frame of Government' in Ireland had collapsed, and that 'Ireland was as a clean paper' – a country
in which his vision of a godly reformed society could be
effected. Here, he believed, was an opportunity to reform
the law – to do 'justice amongst these poor people, which,
for the uprightness and cheapness of it, may exceedingly
gain upon them' – and bring about social justice – to prevent 'injustice, tyranny and oppression from their land-
lords, the great men, and those that should have done
them right'.[20] But Cromwell's main concern, as might be
expected given his treatment of them, was not for the Irish.
With supreme English arrogance he told the Irish clergy in
January 1650 that he had gone to Ireland '(by the assist-
ance of God) to hold forth and maintain the lustre and
glory of English liberties in a nation where we have an undoubted right to do it'.[21] Reformation in Ireland was seen
by Cromwell as 'a good precedent even to England itself',
and when he came back to England he enthused to Edmund Ludlow about 'his intention to contribute his utmost
endeavours to make a thorow reformation of the Clergy
and the Law' in England as he had envisaged could be
done in Ireland,[22] and to Lilburne he promised to 'put
forth all his power and interest he had in the world to
make England enjoy the real fruits of all the army's
promises and declarations'.[23]

What happened to Cromwell in Scotland in 1650–51 reinforced these radical views. The major difference between
these two campaigns as far as Cromwell is concerned is his
attitude to the Irish and Scots. He had no doubts that war

against the Scots was necessary. For months the Commons had been urging him to return from Ireland to prepare to meet the threat from the North, which became urgent in April 1650 when Charles Stuart came to an agreement with those in power in Scotland. In June Charles arrived in Scotland, swearing an oath of loyalty to the Covenant and threatening a Scottish invasion of England and a third English Civil War. Cromwell was clear that it was far better to have a war 'in the bowels of another country [than in] our own',[24] and, when Fairfax refused to lead a pre-emptive strike force against the Scots, Cromwell on 20 June accepted the post with John Lambert and Charles Fleetwood as his subordinate officers. Yet there is little reason to doubt his repeated protestations that 'it hath been our desire and longing to have avoided blood' in Scotland.[25] In the first Civil War he had been forced to oppose the religious intolerance of the Scots, but had recognised that there was a 'unity of spirit' of godly Protestantism between the English and Scots. In the second Civil War he had defeated a Scottish invasion but had conceded that there were some Scots who had opposed that invasion and were 'Christians and men of honour'.[26] What held Cromwell back from the kind of punitive action he had taken at Drogheda and Wexford is that these same men were now in power in Scotland. Therefore, Cromwell put as much effort into a propaganda campaign to win over the Scots as he did into defeating them on the battlefield. A barrage of printed declarations and letters attempted to ween the Scots away from armed opposition and to accept that they shared with the English a common Protestant heritage. 'We do and are ready to embrace as much as doth, or shall be made appear to us to be according to the Word of God. Are we to be dealt with as enemies because we come not to your way? Is religion wrapped up in that or any one form?', argued a Declaration of the Army from Newcastle in July 1650, in tones that could not be more different from the declaration sent to the Irish clergy six months before.[27] 'I beseech you, in the bowels of Christ, think it possible you may be mistaken' in having a monopoly of religious truth, he urged the Scottish General Assembly on 3 August 1650.[28] After his army crossed the Scottish border Cromwell continued to believe that the Scots were 'a people fearing His name, though deceived, and to that end have we offered much love unto such'.[29] Even after his great victory at Dunbar he continued the campaign to win the hearts and minds of the Scots, now using their defeat at that battle as evidence of God's rebuke against them. 'The late blow you received is attributed to profane counsels and conduct', he told the governor of Edinburgh Castle on 12 September. 'Our bowels do, in Christ Jesus, yearn after the godly of Scotland.'[30] He also took part in face-to-face debates with Scottish Presbyterian divines in Glasgow and Edinburgh. 'We were rejected again and again', he wrote to Ireton in September, yet still we begged to be believed that we loved them as our souls', and he continued to hope that the propaganda campaign would succeed.[31]

This perhaps helps to explain why Cromwell's military activities in Scotland were sometimes (as S.R. Gardiner wrote) 'halting and irresolute',[32] and that he was often out-manoeuvred by the Scottish commander, David Leslie. That this was so is often obscured by Cromwell's one undoubted stunning victory in Scotland at Dunbar on 3 September, when his opponents, led by Leslie, outnumbered his forces by two to one, and on the eve of the battle Cromwell had been so fearful of defeat that he had even considered getting his troops away from Dunbar by sea. Yet Cromwell confounded expectations of a crushing defeat by unexpectedly taking the initiative and attacking the Scots early in the morning of 3 September, his army killing (by his own estimate) 3,000 Scottish soldiers and taking 10,000 prisoners. Dunbar (as will be seen) had a major effect on Cromwell's political career; it was less important, however, in bringing about English victory in the war with Scotland. For months after Dunbar, Cromwell's main military strategy – to bring Leslie's forces to battle again – failed. Cromwell's subordinate, John Lambert, had a much more consistently successful career and on two occasions he saved the English cause in Scotland after Cromwellian mistakes: on 2 November 1650 Cromwell's failure to engage the Western Covenanters at Hamilton was followed by Lambert's victory there two days later, which delivered the western Lowlands into English hands; and in July 1651 after Cromwell had failed for months to force the Scottish army into a battle, Lambert did so at Inverkeithing in Fife, killing 2,000 and taking about 1,500 prisoners. As in Ireland, the Cromwellian conquest of Scotland owed not a little to the contribution of his subordinates and the divisions amongst his opponents. It is even far from clear whether, after Inverkeithing, Cromwell planned a strategy which forced Leslie's army to march south into England.[33] He certainly felt it necessary to defend himself to the Commons against having made another tactical error. But it was a strategy, if that is what it was, that worked. His breakneck march south after Leslie and his rendezvous with John Lambert and Thomas Harrison resulted in a decisive victory over Charles II and the Scots at Worcester on 3 September 1651.

Doubts there may be about whether Cromwell's military reputation is fully deserved; there are, however, none about the dramatic radicalising effects that military victories had on him. They were a source of optimism, since he was in no doubt that the victories had been won with God's help, overcoming immense odds. After the victory at Dunbar 'Oliver was carried on as with a divine impulse. He did laugh so excessively as if he had been drunk, and his eyes sparkled with spirits', according to one witness.[34] Dunbar, he exulted, was 'the prospect of one of the most signal mercies God hath done for England and His people' . . . the unspeakable goodness of the Lord'.[35] His faith in providence was renewed. 'My weak faith hath been upheld', he wrote in a rare surviving letter to his wife after Dunbar.[36] The battle of Worcester fought, like Dunbar, on his 'lucky day', 3 September, was 'a very glorious mercy . . . [it] is alone His doing'.[37] Military victories, however, were also a source in Cromwell of great dynamism as well as optimism. They necessitated that God should be repaid for his blessings. 'How shall we behave ourselves after such mercies?', he asked the Reverend John Cotton in Boston, New England.[38] After Dunbar he gave his most explicit answer to date to that question: 'We that serve you beg you not to own us, but God alone', he wrote to the speaker of the Commons on 4 September 1650.

We pray you own His people more and more, for they are the chariots and horsemen of Israel. Disown ourselves, but own your authority, and improve it to curb the proud and the insolent, such as would disturb the tranquility of England, though under what specious pretences soever; relieve the oppressed, hear the groans of poor prisoners in England; be pleased to reform the abuses of all professions; and if there be anyone that makes many poor to make a few rich, that suits not a Commonwealth.[39]

After his last great victory at Worcester on 3 September 1651 Cromwell returned to Westminster determined to press the Rump to become the vehicle for such a reformation.

·   ·   ·

AFTER WORCESTER

When referring in later years to his return to Westminster in September 1651 Cromwell habitually emphasised the great expectations he then had of reformation and his deep sense of disillusion at the way these expectations were dashed.

> After it had pleased God not only to realise Ireland and give in Scotland, but so marvellously to appear for his people at Worcester . . . the Parliament had opportunity to give the people the harvest of all their labour, blood and treasure, and to settle a due liberty both in reference to civil and spiritual things . . . it was a matter of much grief to the good and well-affected of the land, to observe the little progress which was made therin.[40]

What Cromwell did not stress was that for a long period after Worcester he was not simply a dynamic advocate of godly reformation. As in 1647 one of his main aims was to make godly reformation respectable and acceptable to the parliamentary classes. However, his task was, if anything even more difficult now than it had been in 1647. Not only had Pride's Purge made no significant impact on the over-whelmingly conservative political and social character of opinion in the Long Parliament (thanks in part to Crom-well's activities in 1648–49), but hatred of the army had grown enormously since 1647. In the eyes of many MPs the army now stood for the arbitrary use of power against par-liament, as well as for regicide. Cromwell's reform propo-sals consequently suffered by being associated with the hated army.

Despite his absence from Westminster for so long there

is little doubt that Cromwell was well aware of the hostile climate there to the army and reform. On his military campaigns he had received regular reports from correspondents of the Rump's slow progress towards reform. Even civilian republicans in the Rump, like Henry Marten and Thomas Chaloner, shared the hostility to the army and devoted their energies to commercial and foreign affairs. They 'will not suffer to be done things that are so plain as they ought to do themselves', wrote Henry Vane junior to Cromwell in August 1651,[41] and other correspondents complained that, despite the passage on 27 September 1650 of the Toleration Act, which repealed the laws compelling attendance at a national church, the Rump placed more emphasis on repressive measures like the Blasphemy Act (April 1650) and the Adultery Act (May 1650), which reflected the Rump's paranoid fear that religious sects were countenancing excessive sexual and religious licence. The Adultery Act even went as far as prescribing the death penalty for this offence. After Dunbar the only measure of legal reform that was passed was an act making legal proceedings in English statutory, bearing out Cromwell's complaint to Lilburne in June 1650 that 'the sons of Zeruiah are yet too strong for us; and we cannot mention the reformation of the law, but they presently cry out, we design to destroy propriety [property]'.[42]

It is a remarkable testimony to the strength of Cromwell's commitment to working within the existing constitution that he spent eighteen months after Worcester battling against the sons of Zeruiah, attempting to reconstruct a broad-based political alliance at Westminster that would attract enough support to push through reform measures that would satisfy his and the army's expectations. This, of course, was what he had attempted to do in 1647 with a reform programme based on *The Heads of the Proposals* and working with his Political Independent allies. The traumatic events of 'that memorable year', 1648, had shattered that attempt; but it is not surprising that when Cromwell returned to Westminster at the end of 1651 he should try to re-form the political alliance that had been a key one in his political career during the previous ten years. There are many indications that, although many of his old friends were appalled by Cromwell's role in the revolutionary events of December 1648 and January 1649, and refused to take part in the government of the republic, he still kept in touch with them. He corresponded with them when he was away with the army in Ireland and Scotland and, for example, he stayed at William Pierrepoint's house, Rufford Abbey, near Mansfield on 23 August 1651 *en route* for Worcester. Four days later he took time during his headlong dash south to appeal to one of the most powerful of his former allies, Lord Wharton (along with Richard Norton, Thomas Westrowe and Robert Hammond) 'to associate with His people, in His work; and to manifest your willingness and desire to serve the Lord against His and His people's enemies . . . I advise you all in the bowels of love, Let it appear you offer yourselves willingly to His work.'[43]

The refusal of Wharton, Saye and Sele or any of the other Political Independent peers to respond to Cromwell's appeals and to be associated publicly with the republic was a major setback to him after the battle of Worcester. Many of his political associates, such as Sir Gilbert Pickering, Nathaniel Rich, John Carew, Francis Allen, Richard Salwey, Charles Fleetwood and Sir William Masham, were now political lightweights in comparison to Wharton and Saye and Sele. However, many of them had moved in 'middle group'/ Political Independent circles in the 1640s. At least two others, Richard Norton and Thomas Westrowe, who had been absent from parliament since 1648, returned to their seats in the Commons in the autumn of 1651. Above all, two Political Independents, Henry Vane junior and Oliver St John, were very close to Cromwell on his return to London. The influence of St John on Cromwell at this time may have been especially great. He was a member of the parliamentary committee that had talks with the victorious Cromwell at Aylesbury in Buckinghamshire on his journey from Worcester to London. Bulstrode Whitelocke, who was also there, noted that 'my Lord Chief Justice St John [talked] more than all the rest'.[44] He was also present at another meeting in December 1651 in London at the house of William Lenthall, speaker of the Commons, at which Cromwell made plain how close he was to St John's view that 'the Government of this Nation without something of Monarchical power, will be very difficult to be so settled as not to shake the foundation of our Laws, and the

Liberties of the People'. Cromwell called the meeting, attended by army officers (Whalley, Fleetwood, Desborough and Harrison) and MPs (including Whitelocke and Thomas Widdrington) as well as St John, because 'he held it necessary to come to a Settlement of the Nation'. When his fellow army officers argued for a republican settlement, others countered with arguments for a return of monarchy, perhaps, suggested Widdrington, echoing a plan aired in December 1648, in the person of Charles I's younger son, the duke of Gloucester, who was 'too young to have been in arms against us, or infected with the principles of our enemies'. Cromwell's response to that suggestion illustrates that his aims were still very much as they had been in 1647 at the time of the Heads of the Proposals: 'I think, if it may be done with safety, and preservation of our Rights, both as Englishmen and Christians, that a Settlement with somewhat of Monarchical power in it would be very effectual.'[45] During the next fifteen months, he tried his utmost to secure a broad-based acceptance of the regime, as he had done during the negotiations over *The Heads of the Proposals*, by advocating leniency for Royalists. Moreover, he also tried to secure 'the rights' of 'Englishmen and Christians': liberty of conscience for many Protestants, reform of the law, and (last but by no means least) the calling of regular parliaments with representation based on a redistribution of parliamentary seats.

Cromwell was frustrated in each of these aims by the conservative obstructionism of the Rump Parliament. It is true that the Rump passed on 24 February 1652 an Act of General Pardon and Oblivion lifting the threat of legal proceedings against supporters of the king, and its preamble reflected Cromwell's own aim that 'all Rancour and Evil Will occasioned by the Late Differences may be buried in perpetual Oblivion . . . and the former Commotions and Troubles end in a quiet calm and comfortable Peace'.[46] But this intention was vitiated by the many exceptions that were made to the general pardon – 'so many', writes David Underdown, 'that the act's title was seriously inaccurate'.[47] During its passage through the Commons Cromwell often intervened to try to extend its provisions to individual Royalists, as he did in the cases of Charles Cavendish and the earl of Norwich and his son, Lord Goring. Cromwell's orts to curb the vengeance he had encouraged in 1648 id not totally fail. In July 1651 his friend Robert Hammond had urged him to secure a pardon for Christopher Love, a Presbyterian clergyman, who was found guilty of plotting for the restoration of the monarchy. This would, wrote Hammond, be 'a means to unite the hearts of all good men, the best of whose spirits, are set in the ways of the Lord'.[48] Cromwell could not save Love from execution, but he was instrumental in securing in October 1651 a reprieve for his accomplices. However, at the same time he failed to prevent the execution of the earl of Derby for holding the Isle of Man against the republican navy and for supporting Charles II before and at the battle of Worcester. Vengeful Commonwealth MPs, such as Sir Arthur Haselrig, howled for Derby's death, as did the newspaper, *Mercurius Politicus*, which was rapidly becoming the official mouthpiece of the republican government: 'the guilt of bloud . . . is a thing not to be dispenced with by man, and the avenging therof [is] not honourable and agreeable with the Iustice of God and the Parliament'.[49] Moreover, the Rump proceeded to pass three Acts of Sale (in July 1651, August 1652 and November 1652) which named 780 Royalists whose estates were confiscated for sale by Trustees of the Commonwealth.

More irritating for Cromwell was the Rump's barren record on religious toleration, law and parliamentary reform. Increasingly it became clear that there was little substance in the promises many MPs made to pass measures on each of these topics. They seemed keener on passing acts suppressing religious nonconformity than on promoting religious liberty, and their excessive religious intolerance has been noted above. The commission it appointed under Matthew Hale produced a string of proposals for reform of the law, but significantly not one of them was put into effect. Moreover, although Cromwell and St John were successful in the early days after Worcester in getting the Rump to take steps towards arranging its own dissolution and new elections, following the redistribution of seats proposed in *The Heads of the Proposals*, the Rump continually hedged on the difficult question of exactly when it was to be dissolved and be replaced by a new parliament.

On 20 April 1653 Cromwell violently put an end to the

Rump Parliament. After making an angry speech in which he called MPs to their faces, among other things, 'whore-masters', 'drunkards' and 'corrupt and unjust men and scandalous to the Profession of the Gospel', he ordered a small force of musketeers to 'take away those baubles', the speaker's ceremonial mace, and to clear MPs out of the chamber.[50] Why did Cromwell act so militantly? In one sense the explanation is that by now Cromwell was a man whose patience was at breaking point at the repeated failures of the Rump to co-operate with his lengthy political efforts to secure reform slowly but surely by parliamentary means. During the winter months of 1652–53 the Rump's record on reform was particularly barren, and it may be that Cromwell's disillusion with parliament for a time be-came so great that he doubted whether any parliament elected without imposing qualifications on new members would be hostile to reform. Certainly the meeting he had with St John and leading MPs on 19 April 1653 seems to have considered a plan for the dissolution of the Rump to be followed by the appointment of a council of forty MPs and army officers who would hold supreme authority until a new parliament should meet at an unspecified future date. Moreover, it is now fairly certain that 'the bill for a new representative' being considered by the Rump when its proceedings were terminated by Cromwell on the follow-ing day did not provide for the perpetuation of the Rump in power, as has long been thought, but for new elections in the autumn with new MPs vetted by the outgoing parlia-ment. If Cromwell knew that, then his mistrust of parlia-ment's hostile attitude towards the army and reform was greater than has often been realised.

Yet it is likely that it was not just these practical political considerations alone that drove Cromwell to act on 20 April 1653 contrary to his attachment to constitutional re-spectability and to expel the Rump Parliament by force. Ever since he had returned to London after the battle of Worcester, Cromwell had been subjected to a barrage of petitions and letters from those in the army and outside who were anxious to remind him, not only of the refor-ming aspirations he had voiced after Dunbar and Worces-ter, but also that he had a contract with God to put these into effect. 'Great thinges God has done for you in warr',

William Erbury told Cromwell in January 1652, 'and good things men expect of you in peace; to break in peices the oppressor, to ease the oppressed of their burdens, to release the prisoners of their bondes, and to relieve poore familys with bread . . . the poore of the nation are waiting at your gates . . . that there be noe begger in Israel'[51]. Others, too, were not slow to point out the consequences of what would happen if Cromwell broke that contract. 'Remember Hezekiah's fate and judgement', Ireton wrote to Cromwell from Ireland in 1651,[52] referring to the Old Testament leader of Israel whom God had helped defeat Sennacherib, but whose subsequent pride brought God's wrath on him. Only when 'he humbled himself' did God avert his wrath from Hezekiah and his people. As it became increasingly apparent that the Rump's promises to pass reforms were hollow, so Cromwell and the army came more and more to interpret these problems as signs that God's blessings on them had now turned to wrath. In November 1652 a despondent Cromwell was reported to have wondered aloud to Bulstrode Whitelocke 'What if a man should take upon him to be a king?', a comment that is often quoted. Perhaps more important at this time is something else Cromwell said to Whitelocke on the same occasion: 'there is little Hope of a Settlement to be made by them [MPs in the Rump Parliament], really there is not . . . We all forget God, and God will forget us, and render us up to Confusion.'[53] As in April 1648 the Army Council and Cromwell held prayer meetings in January 1653 to seek God's guidance and to find the source of their problems. At one of these prayer meetings the officers concluded that they were failing because they were not doing God's work: 'our hearts have been looking after the things of the world and our present affairs', they wrote in a circular sent to regiments throughout Britain, 'more than the things of Jesus Christ and his People'. For about a month from early March 1653 Cromwell was absent from the Commons and the Council of State, a period of withdrawal and introspection which preceded the dynamic action he took on 20 April and during which he tried to see what was God's will. Even though it comes from such a hostile source as Heath's *Flagellum* there is a ring of truth about what Cromwell is reported to have said when he went to the Commons on 20 April: 'When I went there I did not think to have done this [expel the Rump], but perceiving the spirit of God so strong upon me, I would not consult with flesh and blood at all.'[54] This is not the full story: Cromwell was a skilful, cunning politician who knew that the gulf between parliament and army was now so wide that he would soon have to take the side of the army or risk losing his influence with it. Yet it is likely that on 20 April Cromwell did not act calmly and coolly, but that he was driven by guilt and a desire to regain God's blessing. To that extent the army's declaration of 22 April 1653 that 'we were led by necessity and providence to act as we have done' is an apt comment on what had happened two days before.[55]

. . .

NOTES AND REFERENCES

1. Abbott, vol. II, p. 7.
2. Abbott, vol. II, p. 38.
3. B. Worden, *The Rump Parliament 1649–53* (Cambridge University Press, 1974), pp. 68, 191.
4. *State Papers Collected by Edward Earl of Clarendon* (2 vols, Clarendon Press, 1773), Appendix, p. li.
5. It was the words 'I doe approve of the late acts of the Commons of England assembled in parliament, erecting a high court of justice for the trying and adjudging of Charles Stuart, late King of England' in a motion proposed by Henry Ireton and Henry Marten that caused most offence and were removed. See S. Barber, 'The Engagement for the council of state and the establishment of the Commonwealth government', *Historical Research,* **63**, 1990.
6. Abbott, vol. II, p. 20.
7. S.R. Gardiner thought that these Whitehall debates took place at Cromwell's suggestion, *History of the Great Civil War* (reprint edn, Windrush Press, 1987, 4 vols), vol. IV, p. 238.
8. Abbott, vol. II, pp. 41–2.
9. Abbott, vol. II, pp. 67–8.
10. Abbott, vol. II, p. 39.
11. Abbott, vol. II, p. 38.
12. Abbott, vol. II, p. 107.

13. Abbott, vol. II, pp. 198, 199.
14. Abbott, vol. II, p. 127.
15. Abbott, vol. II, p. 142.
16. Abbott, vol. II, p. 127.
17. Abbott, vol. II, p. 176.
18. Quoted in P.J Corish, 'The Cromwellian conquest, 1649–53' in T.W. Moody, F.X. Martin and F.J. Byrne, (eds) *A New History of Ireland, ii, Earley Modern Ireland 1534–1691* (Clarendon Press, 1976), p. 347.
19. Andrew Marvell, *An Horation Ode Upon Cromwell's Return from Ireland.*
20. Abbott vol. II pp. 187, 273.
21. Abbott, vol. II, p. 205.
22. Abbott, vol. II, p. 273.
23. Abbott, vol. II, p. 277.
24. Abbott, vol. II, p. 270.
25. Abbott, vol. II, p. 325.
26. See pp. 42 and 62.
27. Abbott, vol. II, p. 285.
28. Abbott, vol. II, p. 303.
29. Abbott, vol. II, p. 325.
30. Abbott, vol. II, p. 339.
31. Abbott, vol. II, p. 327.
32. S.R Gardiner, *History of the Commonwealth and Protectorate* (reprint edn, Windrush Press, 1988–9, 4 vols), vol. I, p. 280.
33. See Cromwell's letter to the Speaker of the Commons, excusing his tactics, which may 'trouble some men's thoughts', 4 August 1651, Abbott, vol. II, p. 444.
34. Recorded by John Aubrey, who was told it by 'one that I know, and who was present' at Dunbar, Abbott, vol. II, p. 319.
35. Abbott, vol. II, p. 324.
36. Abbott, vol. II, p. 329.
37. Abbott, vol. II, p. 461.
38. Abbott, vol. II, p. 483.
39. Abbott, vol. II, p. 325.
40. Abbott, vol. II, p. 5.
41. Quoted in Worden, *Rump,* p. 261.
42. Abbott, vol. II, p. 273.
43. Abbott, vol. II, p. 453.
44. Abbott, vol. II, p. 471.

45. Abbott, vol. II, pp. 505–7.
46. C.H. Firth and R.S. Rait (eds), *Acts and Ordinances of the Interregnum 1642–60* (2 vols, 1911), vol. II, p. 566.
47. D. Underdown, *Royalist Conspiracy in England 1649–60* (Yale University Press, 1960), p. 58.
48. *Original Letters,* p. 75.
49. *Mercurius Politicus,* 9–16 October 1651, p. 1140.
50. Abbott, vol. II, p. 642.
51. *Original Letters,* pp. 188–9.
52. Quoted in B. Worden, 'Oliver Cromwell and the sin of Achan' in D. Beales and G. Best (eds), *History, Society and the Churches* (Cambridge University Press, 1985), p. 134.
53. Abbott, vol. II, p. 589.
54. Abbott, vol. II, p. 644.
55. Abbott, vol. III, p. 7.

Chapter 5

CROMWELL AND THE GODLY REFORMATION (1653–54)

The irony of Cromwell using troops against the Long Parliament on 20 April 1653 only eleven years after he had risked life and property to fight for its cause was not lost on contemporaries. 'If Mr Pim were alive again', Dorothy Osborne confided to her lover, William Temple, three days later, 'I wonder what hee would think of these proceedings, and whether this would appeare as great a breach of the Priviledge of Parliament as the demanding of the 5 members.'[1] As he had done at the end of 1648, Cromwell had acted swiftly when he believed that the cause of godly reformation was in danger from the army's parliamentary enemies. Any bill for a new representative proposed by the Rump, he said in July 1653, 'would have thrown away the liberties of the nation into the hands of those who never fought for it'.[2] If the Rump had not been prevented in 1653 'this cause, which the Lord hath so greatly blessed, and bore witness to, must needs languish under their hands, and by degrees, be wholly lost, and the lives, liberties and comforts of His people delivered into their enemies' hands'.[3] In short, Cromwell was again catapulted in April 1653 (as at the end of 1648) by the dictates of providence and necessity into an impulsive, dynamic and authoritarian course of action. As the reports of his meeting on 19 April with MPs and army officers indicate, the idea of setting up some kind of interim body until an elected parliament should meet again was in his mind. But, having expelled the Rump, it is highly unlikely that he had any *clear* idea of what to do next.

. . .

BAREBONES PARLIAMENT

Cromwell was more certain about what he did not want to do. During the hectic weeks after the dissolution of the Rump he vigorously denied that he had acted in order to establish a permanent Cromwellian military dictatorship. 'If you will say that the liberty of the people by these means [the dissolution of the Rump] is stifled', declared a printed Letter written to a 'gentleman in the country' dated 3 May, 'I must tell you again, it is only suspended, 'tis a sword taken out of a mad man's hand, till he recover his senses.'[4] Of course, this and Cromwell's protestations to his first Protectorate Parliament in September 1654 that his chief aim was 'to lay down the power that was in my hands' need to be treated with a large dose of scepticism.[5] But what gives them some credence is that Cromwell does seem to have directed his political energies immediately after the dissolution to finding a way of passing power to others. Even Edmund Ludlow, although now, like many other civilian Rumper 'Commonwealthsmen', appalled at the naked unconstitutional military power Cromwell had displayed in April 1653, conceded that very soon after the dissolution Cromwell sent for Oliver St John to help 'to draw up some instrument of government that might put the power out of his hands'.[6] Other fragmentary evidence also points to Cromwell at this time taking part with some ex-Rumpers (like Walter Strickland, Richard Salwey, John Carew, Sir Gilbert Pickering and Anthony Stapley) and army oficers (especially John Lambert and Thomas Harrison) in a debate, not about whether or not power should be devolved from the army, but about the nature of the body to which power should be devolved. Lambert urged that a council of twelve men should be chosen by the army to rule temporarily to fill the power vacuum created by the dissolution of the Rump; while Harrison reflected the millenarian, apocalyptic excitement felt by some at this time about the possibilities the dissolution had opened up. He advocated that an assembly of about seventy godly men should be chosen by Independent gathered churches, based on the precedent of the Jewish Sanhedrin, and that this body should rule the country until the day, not long hence, felt Harrison and his Fifth Monarchist friends, when King Jesus should return to earth.

When it was announced by Cromwell and the Council of Officers on 30 April that power would be devolved on a Council of State of ten men until a new British 'supreme authority' was called, consisting of nominated men of 'approved fidelity and honesty' from England, Wales, Scotland and Ireland, Lambert withdrew from politics during the next few months, interpreting this as a personal defeat and a triumph for Harrison's brand of ideological millenarianism. But he, and later commentators who have jumped to the same conclusion, were wrong. Harrison's influence on Cromwell can be exaggerated, not only because, as will be seen, he and Cromwell differed fundamentally on the Dutch war, but principally because Cromwell never shared Harrison's ideological Fifth Monarchist millenarianism. Like other militant Protestants Cromwell shared Harrison's concern that government should be in the hands of godly men, as well as the common Puritan belief in the prophecies of the Old Testament that the outcome of the continuing struggle with Antichrist would one day result in the establishment of the millenium, when King Jesus would return to earth to rule. It is now fairly certain that these ideas were held by many English Protestants at this time. What set Fifth Monarchist millenarians apart, however, is that they stressed that Jesus's Second Coming to earth was imminent, and that the subsequent rule of the saints would be established on lines alien to both the ancient constitution of the country, which would be usurped by the rule of an elite on the lines of the Jewish Sanhedrin, and English 'fundamental law', which would be replaced by the Mosaic code.

Even at the height of this heady phase of dynamism and appetite for radical political action, Cromwell did not lose touch with political reality. He realised that an elected parliament was out of the question now because it would undoubtedly be as hostile to the army and to reform as had been the Rump, but he *was* in favour of calling elected parliaments in the future. Although he was not willing to forecast 'how soon God may fit the people for such a thing', yet, he told the nominated assembly when it met in July 1653, 'none can desire it [an elected parliament] more than I';[7] a view echoed in a declaration of the nominated assembly shortly after it met, that 'our posterities . . . we expect still to be governed by successive parliaments'. What also suggests that the Cromwellian initiative in calling a nominated assembly owed little to Harrison is that gathered churches and radical sects had very little say in the choice of those who were to sit in it. About 144 men of 'approved fidelity and honesty' were finally chosen to sit in the new assembly, but of these only fifteen are known to have been recommended by the gathered churches. During May their appointment was kept very closely in the hands of Cromwell and the senior army oficers. The social status and wealth of those chosen was generally lower than those elected to normal seventeenth-century parliaments, but the vast majority of them were gentlemen; some had served in previous parliaments and many had been educated at a university and Inn of Court and were JPs. Ironically the London leather-seller, Praise-God Barebones, from whom the assembly gained its contemporary nickname, 'Barebones Parliament', was not a typical member of it.

Yet this is not to say that Cromwell remained unaffected by the sense of optimistic expectancy that was reflected in letters he received at the time from Independent congregations up and down the country, such as those in Herefordshire who identified him, on the one hand, as 'the instrument to translate the nation from oppression to libertie, from the hands of corrupt persons to the saints', and, on the other hand, themselves as those who 'live to see the dayes, which our fathers longed to see, and reape the harvest of their hopes'.[8] These sentiments were not unlike those voiced by Cromwell at this time: he hoped (according to an army declaration of 22 April) that a nominated assembly would produce 'the fruits of a just and righteous reformation, so long prayed and wished for . . . to the refreshing of all those good hearts who have been panting after those things'.[9] But the most dramatic and fullest example of Cromwell's millenarian expectancy is his remarkable, lengthy speech at the opening of Barebones Parliament on 4 July 1653, which he made with tears (at times) rolling down his cheeks and with the enthusiastic style of a revivalist evangelical preacher. They were, he told them, the legatees of God's blessing. Power 'comes, therefore, to you by way of necessity, by the ways of the wise Providence of God'. He went on:

> I confess I never looked to see such a day as this – it may be nor you neither – when Jesus Christ should be so owned as He is, at this day, and in this work . . . I say, you are called with a high call. And why should we be afraid to say or think, that this may be the door to usher in the things that God has promised; which hath been prophesied of; which He hath set the hearts of His people to wait for and expect? . . . Indeed I do think something is at the door; we are at the threshold.[10]

Recent studies have demonstrated that Barebones Parliament was not the complete failure it is often portrayed as having been.[11] Few of its members were impractical, visionary religious zealots and its meetings were conducted with business-like efficiency: unlike the Rump, it met for six days a week from eight in the morning, and it discussed many moderate, practical and uncontroversial solutions to widely recognised problems of contemporary government, the Church and the law. It spent much time discussing ways to rationalise the revenue system, including the abolition of the hated excise, introduced by John Pym in 1643 as a means of winning the Civil War. Proposals were discussed to replace tithes as a means of securing a salaried, educated Church ministry. Moreover, it established machinery to replace the Church courts for registering births, marriages and deaths, and for executing the probate of wills. Civil marriages, solemnised by JPs, were legalised. In addition, many moderate sensible measures of legal reform were discussed, including the law relating to debtors and ways of making the law more intelligible to laymen. Barebones Parliament passed acts for the relief of creditors and poor prisoners and for regulating the conditions under which idiots and lunatics were kept. The assembly, too, continued the debate begun by the Rump Parliament to bring about a formal union of England and Scotland.

Why, then, did Cromwell rapidly become disillusioned with Barebones Parliament, so that he later looked back on the experience as 'a story of my own weakness and folly?'.[12] Though it was by no means the major cause, Cromwell came to disagree fundamentally with the attitude of many

in Barebones Parliament who shared the Rump's enthusiasm for the war against the Dutch, begun in 1652 as a
means of defeating England's main trading rivals. Others
too, like Harrison and the Fifth Monarchists, saw the war,
despite the Protestantism of the Dutch, as a necessary step
towards an eventual world-wide overthrow of the Catholic
Antichrist. Storms which killed 2,000 Dutch seamen and
destroyed many Dutch ships in November 1652 were seen
by some radical religious groups in England as a sign that
'those that so passionately desire a peace with this country,
may see the error in the work of the Lord; and that he is
ready to deliver this land into their hands, if they continue
their good resolution to extirpate the Whore of Babylon
and idolatory'.[13] Cromwell disagreed, and although exactly
when he decided to try to end the war is not certain, in the
summer and autumn of 1653 he increasingly took a more
active part in negotiations with the Dutch than did representatives of Barebones Parliament and the Council. Cromwell never seems to have gone as far as some on the
Council who proposed a form of union between the two
Protestant powers, but he was in favour of a coalition, following a treaty to end the war. His reported conversation
with some leaders of the Dutch negotiating team, whom he
met apparently accidentally when walking in St James's
Park on 14 July, reflects his aspirations, which were miles
away from the chauvinism of many in Barebones Parliament: 'The interest of this nation and ours too', the Dutch
ambassadors said that Cromwell told them, 'consisted in
the welfare of commerce and navigation. . . . The world
was wide enough for both.'[14]

There were, however, two far more important reasons
why Cromwell became alarmed by the activities of Barebones Parliament than differences over the Dutch war.
The first is that they jeopardised his hopes of reconciling
conservative political opinion to the republic. Although
many in Barebones Parliament were not low-born revol-
utionaries intent on turning the world upside down, they
were largely drawn from the lesser gentry, and this was
seen as being consistent with the recent ejection by the
Commonwealth government of many established
gentlemen from the commissions of the peace and their
replacement by those who were chosen more for their sup-

port for the regime than for their wealth or social status. What heightened the impact of this is the fact that in the early 1650s many propertied gentlemen were extremely frightened that a social revolution destroying property and privilege was about to follow in the wake of the political revolution of 1649. This fear was played upon by popular newspaper entrepreneurs as a means of boosting circulation figures. The activities of groups such as the Ranters, who advocated the abolition of sin and encouraged people to commit adultery and theft, for example, were fully reported (some historians would say invented)[15] by journalists who portrayed them as being much more popular and organised, and therefore a greater threat to the established order than in reality they were. Against this background even moderate reform measures were viewed with alarm by a paranoid gentry fearful that any change presaged a slide towards social revolution. Therefore, when a minority in Barebones Parliament tried to introduce radical, far-reaching measures, these merely confirmed conservative fears. The proposals of a handful of twelve or thirteen Fifth Monarchist members of Barebones Parliament came to be seen as particularly terrifying. They pressed for fundamental reform of the law on Mosaic lines, departing sharply from the English legal common law tradition. Some advocated abolition of the Court of Chancery and some too lobbied for the abolition of tithes and the rights of lay patronage to church livings, which were measures that were seen rightly as attacks on private property rights. In the face of conservative fears at proposals such as these Cromwell's chances of securing the election in the near future of a parliament sympathetic to his vision of godly reformation began to recede.

Second, and probably for Cromwell most important of all in causing him to become disenchanted with Barebones Parliament was the intolerance of fellow Protestants shown by some of its members and their supporters outside. Until now the main threat to Cromwell's hopes of religious liberty had come from those like the Presbyterians who were in favour of a narrow intolerant national Church. Now for the first time Cromwell found himself defending Presbyterians against attacks from religious sects, and he sent deputations that included John Owen, to the City to urge radical preachers to cease their attacks on their fellow Protestants. One of Cromwell's greatest hopes at the beginning of Barebones Parliament had been, as he said in his opening speech on 4 July, that its members would 'have respect unto all, though of different judgments . . . I think if you have not an interest of love for them [Presbyterians] you will hardly answer this of faithfulness to the Saints'.[16] His letter to Charles Fleetwood in Ireland on 22 August reflects his gloom at the failure of some to fulfil that hope. 'Truly I never more needed all helps from my Christian friends than now! . . . Being of different judgments, and of each sort most seeking to propagate their own, that spirit of kindness that is to them all, is hardly accepted of any.'[17] To Cromwell what was happening in Barebones Parliament was not only endangering his hopes of reconciling conservative opinion to the republic, but some of its members were attacking the centrepiece of his hoped-for godly reformation: liberty of religious conscience.

Equally alarming, some of its members also voiced anti-army sentiments, demanding not only the abolition of the excise but of monthly tax assessments also, which would have necessitated the demobilisation of the greater part of the army, and without the army the cause of godly reformation would have disappeared for ever. Four years later Cromwell summarised his view that, if Barebones Parliament had continued, the result would have been 'the subversion of the laws and of all the liberties of the nation, the destruction of the Ministry of this nation in a word the confusion of all things'.[18] It is hard to believe that Cromwell was being truthful when he later in September 1564 said he 'did not know one tittle' of the plans of some moderates in Barebones Parliament to meet early in the morning of 12 December to push through a paper signed by eighty members handing power back to Cromwell and the army; the first he knew of it, he said, was when 'they all came and brought it, and delivered it into my hands'.[19] What is more certain is that Cromwell needed no persuasion to accept the resignation. Nor was he ignorant of John Lambert's busy work in the previous weeks on a new constitution to replace Barebones Parliament. Lambert returned from the North on 19 November and it was probably shortly after that date that he and other army officers came to Cromwell with a draft constitution (as Cromwell reminded a meeting of army officers over three years later) 'with the name of King on it'.[20] Cromwell rejected the idea of King Oliver as he was to do on a more famous occasion in 1657, but he did not stand in Lambert's way in drafting a new constitution.

On the very day after the resignation of Barebones Parliament Lambert read a draft of what became known as the Instrument of Government to a Council of Officers. This was followed by a series of meetings between Cromwell and the Council of Officers, and 'after several days of seeking God and advising therin', a resolution was passed for a Council of twenty-one to be appointed and for Cromwell to be appointed Lord Protector of the British Republic. On 16 December Cromwell was installed as Lord Protector in Westminster Hall, wearing a plain black suit and a cloak, in a curiously down-beat ceremony that perhaps was apt for the installation as ruler of Britain of a man who began life as a farmer on the outer fringes of East Anglian gentry society.

· · ·

THE PROTECTORATE AND THE SEARCH FOR A GODLY REFORMATION

When Cromwell was installed as Protector on 16 December 1653 he swore an oath that asserted that the collapse of Barebones Parliament necessitated that 'some speedy Course should be taken for the Settlement of these Nations [England, Ireland, Scotland] upon such a Basis and Foundation as, by the Blessing of God, might be lasting, secure Property, and answer those great Ends of Religion and Liberty so long contended for'.[21] A major theme of Cromwell's career as Protector is his attempt to reconcile these conflicting aims: to erect a constitutional system that would 'secure Property' and thereby attract the support of the traditional ruling classes of England, and to ensure that 'those great Ends of Religion and Liberty so long contended for' since 1642 were achieved. The temptation facing anyone studying the Protectorate is to follow those who at the time emphasised the first of these aims at the expense of the second. In the mid-1650s an anonymous satirist wrote in very bad verse:

A Protector, what's that? 'Tis a stately thing,
That confesseth itself but the ape of a king
A tragicall Caesar acted by a Clowne;
Or a brass farthing stamp'd with a kind of crown.[22]

Others who have written since Cromwell's death have taken up this same theme, depicting the Protectorate as 'years of retreat, the successive stages in the process of sell-out, by which the monarchy is restored in all but name well before 1660'.[23]

However, the Protectorate did not mark a conservative drift back to the restoration of the monarchy. As will be seen in the next two chapters, Cromwell never lost his commitment to reform to the very end of his life. Indeed in the 1650s his desire for reform may have increased, and at times his anxiety to achieve it led him to become even less scrupulous than he had been in the past about the methods he was willing to use. The main aim of the last section of this chapter is to emphasise the point that, at the beginning of the Protectorate, even though the Instrument of Government and Cromwell's actions and speeches in the months up to the meeting of the first Protectorate Parliament in September 1654 display his yearning for the support of the English landed classes and for constitutional respectability, they also illustrate his sustained desire for godly reformation and throw more light than ever before on what he meant by that vague phrase.

There is no denying that Cromwell as Protector often looked and acted like a king. In the early months of the Protectorate the Council of State ordered that the former royal palaces, St James's, Westminster, Somerset House, Greenwich House, Windsor Castle and Hampton Court, as well as the king's manor house at York, be vested in Cromwell and his successors. In April 1654 Cromwell and his wife and aged mother moved into Whitehall Palace from their lodgings in the nearby Cock-Pit, overlooking St James's Park. From there, like the Stuart monarchs, Cromwell conducted government business during the week, but as time went by at the weekends he stayed at Hampton Court, where, as at Whitehall, he lived in some style. During the Protectorate Cromwell and his Council ordered that lavish tapestries and paintings be re-installed at Hampton Court, including in the Cromwells' bedroom, and that statues and fountains be erected there and in protectoral palaces in London. Sir John Evelyn visited Whitehall in February 1656 after a long absence 'and found it very glorious and well furnished'.[24] Moreover, the Protectorate court soon adopted some of the other outward trappings of regality. Cromwell as Protector was habitually addressed as 'Your Highness' by English courtiers and foreign ambassadors, and certainly by 1656 if not before the Council of State was styled as 'Privy Council'. In his dealings with foreign ambassadors Cromwell was sometimes informal, meeting them on walks in St James's Park or, in the case of the Swedish ambassadors with whom he got on very well, inviting them to spend weekends with him and his family at Hampton Court. But in the main his conduct of foreign affairs was as formal and ceremonial as that of European monarchs. Foreign ambassadors often had to pass through four apartments with closed doors between them before Cromwell finally received them in his 'cabinet' room. As will be seen, Cromwell's re-installation as Protector in 1657 had some of the characteristics of a royal coronation, and in 1658 he even created two life peers: Charles Howard was made Baron Gilsand in July and Edward Dunock Baron Burnell in August.

However, such developments should not be interpreted as conservative milestones on the road to the restoration of the monarchy in 1660. They were certainly not intended to pave the way for the return of the old political order. Rather they were an essential part of Cromwell's desire to pursue the kind of strategies he and his political allies had worked for in the later 1640s. As in the past, an essential key to understanding Cromwell's actions as Protector is the continuing importance to him of the programme he had pursued in 1647 with his Political Independent allies. This explains, first of all, why, as he had in *The Heads of the Proposals* in 1647, he continued to attempt to gain support for the regime by forgetting past divisions. This was one of the key themes of his opening speech to his first Protectorate parliament in September 1654, using a metaphor that often recurs in his writings and speeches. There was a need, he said for 'healing and settling . . . remembering transactions too particularly (at least in the heart of many of you) may set the wound fresh a-bleeding'.[25] In the first few months of the Protectorate many expedients were used to try to heal those wounds. Even the choice of the words 'Lord Protector' as Cromwell's title may have been made in the hope that it would be seen as a reassuring, familiar name from English history, and during the 1650s the word 'Commonwealth' was frequently preferred to 'republic', again perhaps with the same intent. The membership of the Protector's new Council of State may also have been determined with at least one eye to cultivating the support of conservative opinion. One has to write 'may have been', because little or nothing is known about the process by which the new Council was chosen in December 1653. Yet eight of its original fifteen members (Anthony Ashley Cooper, Henry Lawrence, Richard Major, Sir Gilbert Pickering, Francis Rous, Philip Sidney Viscount Lisle, Walter Strickland and Charles Wolseley) were civilians, and only Desborough, Fleetwood, Lambert and Skippon can definitely be catalogued as 'soldiers'. Moreover, the later nominations to the Council of Nathaniel Fiennes (younger son of Lord Saye and Sele) in April 1654 and of Edmund Sheffield, earl of Musgrave, in June 1654 gave the Council an even more marked civilian, conservative complexion. Moreover, Cromwell frequently interfered to protect ex-Royalists, like the earl of Bridgewater in mid-1654, from the vengeance of the sequestration commissioners. In June 1654 he signed an order allowing Lady Tyringham to recover all her family's estates in Ireland that had been lost to parliament in 1642. It is now fairly certain that many Royalists were able to recover, at a financial cost, many of the estates they had lost by confiscation at the hands of the regimes of the 1640s and early 1650s, a point given testimony by contemporary complaints from both ends of the political spectrum. The republican, Edmund Ludlow, was angry that Cromwell instructed assize judges on their circuits of the English provinces to show favour to Royalists, while the Royalist, Edward Hyde, was bemused that 'Cromwell proceeds with strange dexterity towards the reconciling of all kinds of persons, and chooses out those of all parties whose abilities are most eminent. He has sent a pass to Mr Hollis [Denzil Holles], has given Lord Rothes his liberty and estate, and has restored Sir John Stavell to his fortunes'.[26]

One of Cromwell's earliest attempts to woo support for the Protectorate was to abandon the Rump's oath of engagement, which forced men to swear allegiance to the republic and to recognise the abolition of the monarchy and the House of Lords.

Moreover, again as he had done earlier, Cromwell wooed conservative supporters by depicting his regime as one that had rescued the country from social subversion. 'The magistracy of the nation', he asked in September 1654, describing the situation on the eve of the Protectorate, 'was it not almost trampled under foot, under desire and contempt by men of Levelling principles . . . for the orders of men and ranks of men, did not that Levelling principles tend to the reducing all to an equality?' As in 1649 Cromwell raised the Leveller bogeyman; his ex-friend, John Lilburne, was again in the Tower, and Cromwell took great pains to appear as the bastion of the traditional, hierarchical social order, saying in his September 1654 speech to parliament: 'a nobleman, a gentleman, and a yeoman. (That is a good interest of the nation and a great one.)' He even underlined his commitment to safeguarding the social status quo by claiming in that speech that 'property [was one of] the badges of the kingdom of Christ'.[27]

Many of the constitutional provisions of the Instrument of Government, too, reflected aspirations Cromwell had shared with Political Independents in the 1640s. The fundamental basis of the new constitution – government by 'one single person and a Parliament' – followed *The Heads of the Proposals*, as did the insistence that there should be clear limitations on the executive authority of the Protector. Under the Instrument of Government, control of the militia was shared by Protector and parliament, and, above all, the Protector was to rule with the advice of the Council of State. Peter Gaunt's recent work on this institution has emphasised the ways in which it was given a much more prominent role in government than royal privy councils before or since.[28] In the crucial area of finance, the appointments of senior officers of state and control of the armed forces, the Protector had to act with the consent of the Council. Cromwell later (in a speech on 21 April 1657) squealed that these limitations made him like 'a child in its swaddling clothes . . . by the [Instrument of] Govern-

ment, I can do nothing but in ordination with the Council'.[29] That (it will be argued later) is a claim that cannot
be wholly accepted. It is difficult to swallow the view that
Cromwell was a docile constitutional puppet of the Council. But there is no doubt that, in making executive decisions, he had to treat its advice much more seriously than
the sometimes off-hand ways in which his royal predecessors ignored their privy councils.

At the beginning of the Protectorate the difference is
most strikingly apparent in the ways in which decisions
were reached on foreign policy. The ending of the war
with the Dutch, which was finally accomplished by a
treaty signed on 5 April 1654, was carried out with conciliar consent. More interesting are the council debates
that took place in the first spring and summer of the
Protectorate on the vexed question of which side the
British Republic should take in the European super-
power struggle between France and Spain. (Since the
short-lived abortive intervention by Charles I in the mid-
1620s, England had been a mere spectator of this conflict.) As we shall see in the last chapter, pressure on the
Protectorate to abandon its neutrality in international affairs was difficult to withstand. Unfortunately the evidence of the ensuing debates among Cromwell and his
councillors is sketchy and as irritating to historians as it
was to the Venetian ambassador at the time. 'No government on earth discloses its own acts less', he wrote 'than
that of England. They meet in a room approached
through others, without number, and countless doors are
shut. That which favours their interest best is that a very
few persons, at most sixteen, meet to digest the greatest
affairs and come to the most serious decisions.'[30]

But two accounts do survive of debates in April and July
1654, which reveal a split in the council on the question of
whether or not to ally with France in a war against Spain.
As will be seen, Cromwell eventually sided with the majority
anti-Spanish view, and in August the decision (a fateful one
in more than the foreign policy sphere)[31] was taken to
send a combined naval–military expedition to attack Spanish colonies in the Caribbean. Undoubtedly his influence
carried great weight, but 'Cromwell's foreign policy' clearly
was not solely the foreign policy of Oliver Cromwell in the

way that 'Charles II's foreign policy' was the foreign policy of Charles II.

Moreover, the Instrument of Government's provisions for regular parliaments and for elections based on reformed constituencies were also very much influenced by Political Independent aspirations of the 1640s, as well as by the proposals that had been made in the Rump Parliament. Parliaments were to be elected every three years and to sit for a minimum of five months, and provisions were made for local officials to send out writs to summon a new parliament if the central government failed to do so. These clauses of the Instrument mark Cromwell's continuing commitment to the cause of parliamentary liberties, which had driven him to fight and risk his life in 1642. There are no grounds for believing that Cromwell's statement to parliament in September 1654 was solely an act of cynical calculation. When he said, 'a free parliament . . . is that which I have desired all my life. I shall desire to keep it so above my life', he was restating a principle he had held since the beginning of his political career in 1640.[32]

But Cromwell's aims at the beginning of the Protectorate were not simply a replication of those of 1647. Many dramatic events had happened in the intervening period that could not fail but leave an impact on his attitudes. Above all, committed though he was to them, 'free parliaments' in the recent past (whether that term was applied to the Long Parliament before or after it was purged in 1648) had shown that they were sometimes hostile to other causes that Cromwell held dear, especially to the army and to godly reformation. This accounts for a major feature of the Instrument of Government that, unlike others, marks a clear break with Cromwell's Political Independent inheritance. Running through the new constitution is an intense distrust of parliaments. This is reflected above all in two major incursions made by the drafters of the Instrument into parliamentary liberties: the right given to the council to exclude elected MPs at the beginning of each session, and the power given to Protector and Council to legislate before parliament next met. Again, as on other occasions in the past, the paradox of Cromwell's career is clear: a man who had risked his life for parliamentary liberties now accepted a constitution that infringed those liberties in ways that no monarch (with the possible exception of Charles I) had done. Cromwell's desires for 'healing and settling' and for constitutional respectability for his regime was prominent at the inauguration of the Protectorate, but it by no means swamped his determination to secure a godly reformation.

What did Cromwell mean by that vague phrase? Of all the problems that make up the enigma of Cromwell's whole political career this is the one that is the most difficult to resolve, largely because Cromwell never gave a clear and specific definition of what he understood by godly reformation. Although, as has been seen, the hope of reform is a recurring theme in his speeches and letters during the Civil War and after (and was to continue to be apparent in the 1650s) more often than not he described his hopes in very general terms. His desire to secure 'the good things' or 'to reap the fruits of all the blood and treasure that had been spent in this cause' are typically vague Cromwellian references to his goal.

It is certainly easier to say what Cromwell's vision of a reformed society was *not* than what it was. Emphatically it was not hostile to fun and enjoyment, nor was it incompatible with the flowering of music, art and literature. All too often the available sources about Cromwell's life are 'public' and 'official' ones that reveal little about the 'private' man. But occasionally they do reveal glimpses of someone quite unlike the image many have of him as a dour, solemn, 'puritanical' man: a Cromwell who wore his hair long, had a sense of humour, danced, drank alcohol and smoked tobacco. Sometimes his sense of fun was fairly crude, as it was at his daughter Frances's wedding to Robert Lord Rich in November 1657, when he was reported to have thrown wine over the dresses of the women guests and 'dawbed all the stools where they were to sit with wet sweet-meates', but the wedding celebrations (on the day after the formal ceremony) included music by '48 violins and 50 trumpets, and much mirth with frolics, besides mixt dancing' until the early hours of the next morning.[33] Whitelocke records a revealing picture of Cromwell at his ease with his intimate councillors, when he 'would sometimes be very familiar with us, and by way of diversion, would make verses with us, and every one must try his fancy; he commonly called for tobacco pipes and a candle, and would now and then take tobacco himself . . . '.[34] Even James Heath in his hostile Restoration biography admitted that Cromwell 'was a great lover of music and entertained the most skilfull in that science in his pay and family . . . generally he respected (or at least pretended) [Heath obviously could not resist the snide comment] a love to all ingenious and eximinous [choice] persons in any arts, whom he arranged to be sent or brought to him'.[35] He employed a master of music, James Hingston, in his household in the 1650s, and his patronage and employment of artists, poets and dramatists is well-attested enough to despatch the image of Cromwell the cultural philistine to the historical dustbin. Nor did Cromwell's godly reformation envisage the dismantling of the old social order. On the contrary, the essence of it was that it should take place within it and (as has been seen) Cromwell always maintained a firm opposition to those who threatened to turn the social world upside down.

In one sense Cromwell's failure to be precise about his constructive intentions is not surprising. During his public career since 1640 he had demonstrated that he was not a reflective thinker; rather he fed off the ideologies of others. At all the crucial points in his career before he became Protector he had at his side mentors who worked out in detail ideas which provided the intellectual framework for his actions: St John and Saye and Sele in the immediate aftermath of the Civil War, his son-in-law Henry Ireton at the height of the crisis of 1648–49, St John after the battle of Worcester in the winter of 1651–52, and Harrison and Lambert during the political turmoil of 1653. He often acted impetuously in moments of political crisis and worked out exactly what to do afterwards. There is a danger of imposing a coherent pattern on Cromwell's reforming ambitions that was not there. It is, however, a risk that must be taken in order to make clearer his priorities as Protector.

Two main reforming themes recur in Cromwell's speeches and writings; both were not novel in the mid-seventeenth century but were aspirations that had been sporadically voiced in England by a minority for decades. The first is rooted in ideas developed by 'commonwealth' writers of the 1530s who accepted the notion that the nation (like the human body) was made up of parts of unequal importance. This was not simply a conservative ideology designed to buttress the social status quo; it was also one which spelled out the duties and responsibilities of everyone within the commonwealth. The poor had a duty to work and to obey their social superiors, and those with wealth, as well as having privileges, had responsibilities to care for those less fortunate than themselves. Like the 'commonwealthmen' of the 1530s, Cromwell too considered social justice as an integral part of the ideal society he wanted to create. It was a concern given a great boost by his military experiences, as has been seen. As the war progressed he came to believe that after the war he should secure a just reward for those who had fought with him on the battlefields of Britain: a land fit for heroes to live in. The most explicit reference to this 'commonwealth' strand in Cromwell's aspirations is in his letter (already quoted)[36] that he wrote immediately after the battle of Dunbar in September 1650. 'If there be any that makes many poor to make a few rich that suits not a Commonwealth' was not a clarion call to turn the world upside down, but to ensure that the few who were rich cared for, rather than oppressed, the vast majority who were poor.

Cromwell's concern for social justice manifested itself in his interest in reform of education, government and the law. He did not give educational reform a high priority, but his support for those who attempted to establish a third English university at Durham in the 1650s has rightly been given a lot of publicity, as has his call for the reform of local government. He shared the belief of Charles I and his ministers in the early 1630s that it was not new laws that were needed, but rather ways of ensuring that the existing laws were put into effect. 'We had indeed many and good laws', he said in March 1656, 'yet we have lived rather under the name and notion of a law than under the thing, so that 'tis resolved to regulate the same (God assisting), oppose who will.'[37] Later in April 1657 he made a similar point, emphasising that the failure to achieve social justice was due to a lack of administrative vigour on the part of local magistrates rather than to a dearth of good laws. 'Though you have good laws against the common country disorders that are everywhere, who is there to execute them?', he asked in a speech in April 1657. 'Really a Justice of the Peace shall from the most be wondered at as an owl, if he go but one step out of the ordinary course of his fellow Justices in the reformation of these things.'[38]

Yet Cromwell gave much more emphasis to achieving social justice by reform of the law than by educational and governmental changes. Thurloe, who knew Cromwell as well as anyone, wrote to Whitelocke in 1654 that 'the reformation of the law and the ministry' was Cromwell's chief preoccupation.[39] There is no doubt that he shared the enthusiasm of those army comrades who (according to John Cook, the regicide) said in 1655 that 'law reform [was the] one great thing that . . . they fought for'.[40] As has been seen, the snail-like progress of the Rump on law reform was a major reason why he became deeply disillusioned with parliamentary processes by April 1653. When he addressed parliament again in September 1654, he made a big point of emphasising the concern he had had for law reform in the nine months since he became Protector. He had (he said) 'desired to reform the laws . . . and called together eminent persons . . . to consider how the laws might be made plain and short, and less chargeable to the people, how to lessen expense, for the good of the nation'.[41] To that end in the early months of the Protectorate he had called to London a provincial lawyer from Gloucestershire, William Sheppard, who had already made a name for himself in print as a reforming lawyer and also as a man who shared Cromwell's religious views. It was Sheppard who had a prominent role in drafting the ordinance that Cromwell and his Council issued in August 1654, making access to the court of Chancery easier and cheaper. This was a small enough step forward compared with the massive programme of legal reform measures mapped out by the Hale commission in 1652, but perhaps reform at a moderate pace had a more permanent chance of success than the hasty and divisive progress threatened by the reformers in Barebones Parliament.

If the 'commonwealth' idea of social justice was one integral part of what Cromwell meant by 'godly reformation', another – and undoubtedly for him more important – strand was the concern to extend the Reformation begun in the sixteenth century by bringing about a reformation within the hearts and minds of every individual. As has been seen Cromwell differed from those like Harrison who envisaged the godly reformation being brought about by a dramatic change in government involving rule by a select elite of godly men until the imminent reign of King Jesus in person. In his speech to parliament on 4 September 1654 Cromwell described that prophecy as 'the mistaken notion of the Fifth Monarchy [Men]', and he proposed instead 'a notion I hope we will all honour, wait and hope for, that Jesus Christ will have a time to set up his reign in our hearts, by subduing those corruptions and lusts and evils that are there, which reign now more in the world than, I hope, in due time they shall do'.[42] Just as he drew on 'commonwealth' ideals of social justice, so too Cromwell's vision of an inner reformation – a 'reformation of manners' – was one that had been pursued by godly men and women since at least the 1580s. For them and for Cromwell the Reformation would not be completed until the campaign against individual wickedness – drunkenness, swearing, sabbath-breaking, blasphemy, adultery and sexual immorality – had been completed. Only when this true Reformation had made substantial progress would the country gain God's blessing.

Like his godly comrades, Cromwell believed that the main way of achieving the true reformation was by an alliance of godly magistrates and a reformed ministry, and that the main function of the magistrate should be to ensure that church ministers were educated and godly men, suited to their evangelical role of leading their parishioners towards moral and spiritual reformation. It is not surprising, therefore, that Cromwell's and the Council's major reforms in the first months of the Protectorate were designed to ensure that suitable church ministers were appointed and that unsuitable ones were ejected. That was the aim of two ordinances issued in 1654. One in March 1654 established a central commission of thirty-eight men (who came to be known as 'Triers') who were to assess all applicants for church livings to ensure (as Cromwell later said) that they were 'men of known integrity and piety, orthodox men and faithful'.[43] This was followed in August 1654 by an ordinance which set up commissioners in each county (who came to be called 'Ejectors') who were to weed out ministers guilty of 'ignorance, insufficiency, scandal in their lives and conversations or negligence in their respective callings and places'.

This attempt to make the ministry the spearhead of the reformation of manners, was not, however, Cromwell's main concern. It was a means towards his main aim, which (as has been seen many times already) was to provide 'no compulsion [in religion] but that of light and reason'. His main aim was to erect a loose framework of state control within which individuals could find God for themselves. 'To be a seeker', he had written in October 1646 in a letter to his daughter Bridget, 'is to be of the best sect next to a finder, and such an one shall every faithful seeker be at the end. Happy seeker, happy finder.'[44] Was, then, Cromwell 'a man ahead of his time', 'a champion of modern religious toleration'?

It is important to stress that that is not an apt description of him. Cromwell's definition of religious liberty was a limited one from the very beginning of his public career and remained so until the end of his life in two important respects. The first is fairly obvious: Cromwell made it clear in the Instrument of Government (and on many other occasions) that toleration should not be extended to 'popery or prelacy [nor] to such as, under the profession of Christ, hold forth and practise licentiousness' and those 'that abuse the liberty to the civil injury of others and to the actual disturbance of the public peace'. As will be seen (especially in the cases of Biddle and Nayler) Cromwell was not unwilling, in practice as well as in theory, to exclude some people, including some Protestants as well as Catholics, from the enjoyment of religious liberty. The second limitation on Cromwell's definition of religious liberty is less obvious and has not always been fully appreciated. Cromwell's godly reformation was not intended to bring about religious plurality. His ideal was the maintenance of Protestant unity within a national Church. As will be seen, Cromwell supported the readmittance of Jews to England in 1655, not because of a commitment to universal religious tolerance but because he (in common with many Protestants) believed that the conversion of the Jews was a necessary, essential preliminary to the establishment of the

110

unity of godly people. Equally as important, he denounced the growth of the sectarian fragmentation of Protestantism. Ironically as a man who had been since 1644 smeared by his enemies, such as the earl of Manchester, as 'the darling of the sectaries', he abhorred sectarianism because it was subversive of his ideal of Protestant unity. During the Civil War he had said that 'Presbyterians, Independents all had the same spirit'. In his speech to parliament in September 1654 he restated the point and lambasted those sects which 'saith, Oh! Give men liberty. But give [them] it, and to [their] power [they] will not yield it to anybody else.'[45] Cromwell was not 'a man ahead of his time' looking forward to the collapse of religious uniformity and the rise of religious diversity, but rather he was looking backwards to the restoration of a Church that had more in common with the Church of Elizabeth I and James I than that of Restoration England, in which dissenting religious groups were, albeit reluctantly and under severe penalties, given legal recognition. In March 1654 he appointed a day of fasting and prayer for an end to 'faction' and to bring about 'brotherly love' and a 'healing spirit'.[46] As he had done in Scotland in 1650–51, he debated with intolerant protestant religious groups in England, arguing the case for a universal brotherhood of the godly, campaigning against separate denominational development.

Cromwell's 'toleration' was limited when looked at from a modern standpoint. Nevertheless it is important to stress that he was willing to allow a much greater diversity of religious forms to exist than any other seventeenth-century English government before or after him. For Presbyterians, Independents and Baptists, who were to be savagely persecuted after 1660, Cromwellian England was a haven of religious freedom. 'If men will profess – be those under Baptism, be those of the Independent judgement simply, and of the Presbyterian judgement – in the name of God encourage them . . . to make use of the liberty given them to enjoy their own consciences', he said to parliament in September 1656 in a speech which is one of the clearest definitions of his religious goal:

For . . . undoubtedly this is the peculiar interest all this while contended for. [That] men that believe in

Jesus Christ . . . men that believe the remission of sins through the blood of Christ and free justification by the blood of Christ, and live upon the grace of God, that those men that are certain they are so, are members of Jesus Christ and are to him as the apple of his eye'.

And he added, emphasising that his central concern was with inner beliefs not outward forms of Church government, that this included 'whoever hath this faith, let his form be what it will if he be walking peaceably without the prejudicing of others under another form'.[47]

Moreover, not only did Cromwell's desire for an extension of religious liberty of conscience make him unusual among seventeenth-century rulers of Britain, it also set him apart from many of his contemporaries. Ever since the later sixteenth century, the cause of godly reformation had been a minority one. Godly Puritans were vociferous in later sixteenth- and early seventeenth-century England, but were never more than a tiny minority. Moreover, it is likely that during the 1640s and 1650s, many Puritan gentlemen who had once shared Cromwell's hopes that there might be a godly reformation abandoned that cause as it became associated with army revolt, regicide and threats to turn the world upside down. What makes Cromwell interesting (and at the same time helps to explain the future course of his career and the mountainous political difficulties he faced as Protector) is that he, unlike many others, did not shy away from godly reformation. On the contrary, during the 1650s his commitment to it seems to have become greater and greater.

That Cromwell did not abandon godly reformation is the strongest argument against those who accuse him of self-aggrandisement. Why, then, did he not take a course that would have sent him spinning along the road towards supreme power, enthusiastically supported by the politically powerful parliamentary classes of the country? The explanation is partially rooted in his experiences in the army from 1642–46, in 1648, and from 1649 to 1651. One of the principal effects that these experiences had on him was to distance him from those who had not fought and who had not shared the feeling of brotherhood-in-arms that developed in the New Model Army on its campaigns in England, Ireland and Scotland. Cromwell's memories of his military experiences remained alive and were a major influence on his thoughts and actions throughout his life. What reinforced this influence as a vital one in his career is that (as has been seen) from about the middle of the Civil War he became convinced that what was happening to him and the army were signs that he had a divine, providential mission to bring about a godly reformation. In order to explain this he drew on a biblical parallel that was used very frequently by godly Protestants in England, comparing the struggle of those in post-Reformation England against Catholicism, indifference and immorality with the plight of the Old Testament Israelites who fought for freedom against Egyptian subjection. For godly protestants like Cromwell the Old Testament story of the Israelites had a powerful fascination, and they knew by heart the details of it, of the Israelites fleeing from Egyptian bondage and their miraculous escape, led by Moses, as the Red Sea parted to let them across into the desert – the wilderness – where they lived for forty years until they successfully overcame their enemies in battle at Jericho, and finally settled in Canaan, the Promised Land. But, as the Bible story makes clear, this was only made possible after the Israelites in the wilderness expiated their sins and won God's blessing. Cromwell referred to this directly in his speech to parliament in September 1654, which came after a sermon in which MPs were 'told . . . of a people brought out of Egypt towards the land of Canaan, but, through unbelief, murmuring, repining, and other temptations and sins, wherewith God was provoked, they were fain to come back again and linger many years in the wilderness before they came to the place of rest'. His next sentence makes it clear that, for him, this was a parable for what was happening to England and himself: 'we are thus far through the mercy of God', he said. 'We have cause to take notice of it, but we are not brought into misery; but as I said before, a door of hope is open.' As Cromwell saw it, the English had escaped the bondage of the rule of Charles I and Archbishop Laud, had crossed the Red Sea of Civil War and regicide, and they were now in the wilderness. God had brought them this far and had helped them win great victories over their enemies. The most important question facing Cromwell at the beginning of his Protectorate was whether God would allow them to go further into the Promised Land. For Cromwell in 1654 (and later as will be seen) the answer was clear: only if the English, like the Israelites, first expiated their sins, showed themselves to be morally pure and so won God's blessing. When he addressed MPs at the opening of his first Protectorate parliament in September 1654 he warned them that 'you are not yet entered [into the door of hope but] if the Lord's blessing and his presence go along with the management of affairs at this meeting, you will be enabled to put the top-stone to his work, and make the nation happy'.[48] It is a measure of the determined optimism that Cromwell's providential interpretation of England's recent history gave him that he thought his listeners in parliament would share his visionary aim of erecting a commonwealth characterised by social justice and godly moral reformation.

· · ·

NOTES AND REFERENCES

1. G.C. Moore Smith (ed.), *The Letters of Dorothy Osborne to William Temple* (Oxford, 1928), p. 39.
2. Abbott, vol. II, p. 60.
3. Abbott, vol. II, p. 6.
4. Quoted in A. Woolrych, *Commonwealth to Protectorate* (Oxford University Press, 1982, paperback edn, 1986), p. 110. Woolrych suggests that that author may be John Hill, a journalist employed by Cromwell.
5. Abbott, vol. III, p. 454.
6. Ludlow, *Memoirs*, vol. I, pp. 357–8.
7. Abbott, vol. II, p. 64.
8. *Original Letters*, p. 92.
9. Abbott, vol. III, p. 7.
10. Abbott, vol. III, pp. 63–4.
11. The best and fullest is Woolrych, *Commonwealth to Protectorate*.
12. Abbott, vol. IV, p. 489.
13. Quoted in Woolrych, *Commonwealth to Protectorate*,, p. 324.
14. Abbott, vol. III, p. 73.
15. One who has done so is J.C. Davis, *Fear, Myth and History: The Ranters and Historians* (Cambridge University Press, 1986).

16. Abbott, vol. II, p. 62.
17. Abbott, vol. III, p. 89.
18. Abbott, vol. IV, p. 489.
19. Abbott, vol. III, pp. 454–5.
20. Abbott, vol. IV, p. 418.
21. Abbott, vol. III, pp. 136–7.
22. Quoted in Ivan Roots, *The Great Rebellion 1642–60* (Batsford, 1965), p. 210.
23. W. Lamont, 'The Left and its past: revisiting the 1650s', *History Workshop*, **23**, 1987, p. 142, referring to Christopher Hill's views of the 1650s.
24. E.S. Beer (ed.), *The Diary of John Evelyn* (Clarendon Press, 1955. 6 vols), **11**, p. 166.
25. Abbott, vol. III, p. 435.
26. Edward Hyde, Earl of Clarendon, *History of the Rebellion* (6 vols, ed. W. Macray, 1888) vol. II, p. 323.
27. Abbott, vol. III, pp. 435, 438.
28. See Bibliographical Essay.
29. Abbott, vol. III, p. 488.
30. Quoted in P. Gaunt, 'The "single person's confidants and dependants"? Oliver Cromwell and his protectoral councillors', *Historical Journal*, **32**, 1989, p. 548.
31. See pp. 132–6, 152.
32. Abbott, vol. III, p. 444.
33. Abbott, vol. IV, pp. 661–2.
34. Abbott, vol. IV, p. 462.
35. Quoted in R. Sherwood, *The Court of Oliver Cromwell* (1977), pp. 135–6.
36. See pp. 79–80.
37. Abbott, vol. IV, p. 112.
38. Abbott, vol. IV, p. 494.
39. Quoted in Nancy L. Matthews, *William Sheppard: Cromwell's Law Reformer* (Cambridge University Press, 1984), p. 37.
40. Quoted in D. Veall, *The Popular Movement for Law Reform 1640–60* (Oxford University Press, 1960), p. 73.
41. Abbott, vol. III, p. 439.
42. Abbott, vol. III, p. 437.
43. Abbott, vol. IV, p. 495 (speech of 21 April 1657).
44. Abbott, vol. I, p. 416.
45. Abbott, vol. III, p. 459.
46. Abbott, vol. III, pp. 225–8.

47. Abbott, vol. III, pp. 271–2.
48. Abbott, vol. III, p. 442.

Chapter 6

PARLIAMENT AND PERSONAL RULE
(September 1654 – September 1656)

W.C. Abbott described the establishment of the Protectorate as 'a new and powerful dictatorship'.[1] Any attempt like
this to fit Cromwell into the stereotype of a military dictator ultimately fails to convince. Although Cromwell's break
with the constitutionally correct Political Independents in
1648 was final, he nevertheless remained attached to many
aspects of their political programme and he never seems to
have abandoned the hope of returning one day to the path
of constitutional respectability by ensuring the elections of
regular, free parliaments. His optimism that the Protectorate parliament that met in September 1654 would be the
first of many was at least partly founded on the sense of
relief he felt, as a man who had fought for parliamentary
liberties in the 1640s. It must have seemed to him that the
Instrument of Government had found a way of avoiding,
not only the arbitrary and unlimited rule of one person,
but also the exercise of sole power by a parliament whether
elected like the Rump or nominated like Barebones Parliament. The new constitution, he argued in January 1655 at
the dissolution of the first Protectorate parliament, was 'the
most likely to avoid the extremes of monarchy on the one
hand, and democracy on the other, and yet not to found
dominium in gratia', i.e. a Fifth Monarchy-type constitution in which an elect few claimed to rule as an interim
government until King Jesus should return to earth.[2] It is
not unlikely that Cromwell welcomed his first elected
parliament in 1654 as a means of reviving middle
group/Political Independent strategies combining reformation and settlement. The first part of this chapter
examines the main reasons why this proved impossible

117

and why Cromwell's first Protectorate parliament was for him a complete disaster.

The second part deals with Cromwell's reactions to that failure. The barren record of his first parliament made clear the dilemma he faced as ruler of Britain. He had failed to give the people 'what pleases them' by constitutional means. His reaction was to embark on an authoritarian course of 'giving the people what's good for them'. Indeed many aspects of Cromwell's rule in 1655–56 show a lack of concern for constitutional legality that gives support to those who would depict Cromwell as a military dictator. Moreover, he underwent a personal, spiritual crisis in that period which caused him to be more than ever determined to take England, *via* the rule of the major-generals, into the New Jerusalem – if necessary, by the scruff of its neck. Yet, what is striking about Cromwell is that, even when his iron-fisted authoritarianism was most prominent, he showed that he had not totally abandoned either his Political Independent instincts for 'healing and settling' or his aspirations to secure broad-based support for his regime from the parliamentary classes of the country.

.   .   .

THE FIRST PROTECTORATE PARLIAMENT
SEPTEMBER 1654 – JANUARY 1655

When he dissolved his first parliament in January 1655 Cromwell told MPs that 'when I first met you in this room [on 4 September 1654] it was to my apprehension the hopefullest day that ever mine eyes saw, as to the consideration of the world'.[3] The task he gave them was a mammoth one. 'You have upon your shoulders', he told them when they assembled, 'the interests of the three great nations, with the territory belonging to them . . . you have upon your shoulders the interests of all the Christian people in the world . . . you have great works upon your hands.'[4] When he dismissed them, a bare five months later, his high hopes had turned to bitter anger. They had, he berated them on 22 January 1655, spent most of their time attacking the Instrument of Government, instead of proceeding 'to have made those good and wholesome laws which the people expected of you'. Instead of pursuing the cause of reformation, they had indulged in lengthy constitutional debates and discussions. 'If it be my liberty to walk abroad in the fields, or to take a journey, yet it is not my wisdom to do so when my house is on fire', he said, as he sent them packing.[5] Why did Cromwell's first parliament prove to be such a disappointment to him?

The answer illustrates much about Cromwell's conception of his role as Protector, as well as the daunting opposition he faced, not only from his ex-allies but also from wide sections of influential political opinion in England. Cromwell himself was partly to blame for parliament's failure to push ahead as he hoped with reformation, since he seems to have paid little attention to managing parliamentary proceedings. Some sort of intervention was probably more necessary than ever in this parliament since the redistribution of parliamentary seats under the Instrument of Government had produced a more independent-minded House of Commons than was usual. The new constitution included a major shake-up of parliamentary constituencies in an attempt to relate representation in parliament more accurately to wealth, as had been envisaged in earlier, abortive schemes discussed by army officers and MPs since 1647. As a result the number of MPs elected by counties, as opposed to boroughs, increased, reducing the opportunities for anyone to influence the outcome of elections. Furthermore, the vote was restricted to those with £200 in real or personal property, and the parliament that met in September 1654 reflected probably more fully than ever before the opinions of the substantial landed gentry of the country, which, as has been seen, were running strongly against the army. These opinions were influenced by fears of social and religious radicalism. Yet Cromwell seems to have shown a marked lack of interest in attempting to woo the newly elected MPs. What preparations were made in the weeks before the new parliament met were initiated by the Council rather than the Protector. It was the Council that, in an attempt to win support for the regime, cut the monthly assessment from £120,000 to £90,000 and which, using the powers given it by the Instrument of Government, excluded about eight MPs from sitting. Moreover, when parliament met, MPs were not given any front-bench leadership by the Protector or the councillors who sat in parliament. At the opening of the session Cromwell failed to spell out to MPs the programme of measures he wanted them to put into effect. As has been seen his references to reform were very general indeed. Moreover, Cromwell's councillors in the Commons seem to have made no attempt to guide MPs towards specific reform measures. It is difficult to believe that the reason for all this is Cromwell's political inexperience. As has been seen, ever since at least 1644 there had been many occasions when he had shown himself more than adept at political manipulation and behind-the-scenes wheeling and dealing. The reason seems to have been the role he decided to adopt as Protector as a 'good constable to keep the peace of the parish',[6] in political affairs as in the religious life of the country, merely keeping the peace in order to allow others to pursue the path towards godly reformation. He seems to have made a conscious decision not to intervene in parliament's proceedings. He even later boasted of the fact that after 12 September MPs 'had no manner of interruption or hindrance of mine'.[7]

But the speed and ferocity with which Cromwell's position as Protector was attacked in parliament suggests that, even if Cromwell had not adopted a non-interventionist, 'good constable', approach to parliamentary management, he would still have faced an unco-operative parliament. The main reason is not difficult to see, given the fact that some clauses of the Instrument of Government represented a major attack on parliamentary liberties and that some MPs, notably those republican members like Thomas Scot and Sir Arthur Haselrig, were still smarting at the army's outrageous dissolution of the Rump only seventeen months earlier. The first week of the session was almost wholly taken up with debates in which speaker after speaker, led by republican MPs, attacked one of the key features of the Instrument of Government – the sharing of power between a single person and parliament – and many proposed instead that the supreme authority should be vested solely in the people in parliament. Cromwell's claims that he ruled with God's blessing were dismissed by one speaker with the biting comment that 'the providences of God are like a two-edged sword which may be used both ways'; military victory could well prove that 'the Grand Turk may make a better title than any Christian princes'.[8]

A feature of Cromwell's political career is the bitterness felt against him by those who had once been his allies, who considered that he had been driven by selfish ambition to have abandoned the parliamentary cause. This was certainly the case now, and so violent and sustained was the blast of hatred directed at him by republican MPs that Cromwell was stung into making a dramatic intervention on 12 September, forcing MPs to sign a 'Recognition' of adherence to the principle of government by a single person and parliament, or to withdraw from Westminster.

As a result about a hundred MPs, including the prominent republican MPs, chose the latter course. It is a measure of Cromwell's political isolation, however, that parliament became no more co-operative after the purge of 12 September. In a speech on that day, justifying his intervention, he went on to outline four 'fundamentals' of government: that the country should be governed by a single person and parliament; that parliaments should not be permanent but should be elected frequently; that there should be liberty of conscience in religion; and that the control of the militia should be shared by Protector and parliament. During the remainder of the first Protectorate parliament the last two 'fundamentals' became the focus of attack. Often in accounts of this period the politics of the Long Parliament of the later 1640s, of the Rump Parliament between 1649 and 1653, and of the Protectorate parliaments are treated as separate, discrete episodes. This can be misleading, because there was much continuity of personnel and attitudes running through the parliamentary politics of the later 1640s and 1650s. Many MPs sat in the Long Parliament before and after Pride's Purge and in the Protectorate parliaments. Moreover, distrust of religious liberty and of the army was as marked in Cromwellian parliaments as it had been in parliaments before 1653.

The only major change is that, if anything, the fear that any relaxation of the laws imposing religious uniformity would lead to social subversion had by the early 1650s become more intense than ever. The orchestrated press campaign to vilify unorthodox religious groups, which used the Ranters as bogeymen to try to buttress attachment to religious orthodoxy, continued unabated, and was supported both inside and outside parliament. At the end of

1654 a petition to parliament from the City of London demanded the imposition of religious uniformity, and in December parliament voted unanimously in favour of restraining 'atheism, damnable heresies, popery, prelacy, licentiousness and profaneness'. Parliament even voted, by a majority of one, to establish a committee with the impossible task of enumerating those 'damnable heresies' that should be punished. Moreover, on 13 December it sent John Biddle to the Gatehouse Prison and ordered his books, in which he argued against the divinity of Christ, to be burned by the common hangman.

Later events were to show that Cromwell had little sympathy for Biddle's religious views. In September 1655 Biddle was imprisoned on the Scilly Isles and Cromwell swept aside his attempt to claim immunity under the Instrument of Government with the comment 'that the liberty of conscience provided for in these articles [of the Instrument of Government] should never, while he had any interest in the government, be stretched so far as to countenance those who denied the divinity of our Saviour'.[9] However, there are grounds for believing that Cromwell held back from endorsing fully the parliamentary condemnation of Biddle in 1654. As in a much more famous (because better-reported) case in 1656, that of the Quaker James Nayler, the Biddle case highlighted the fact that the intolerance directed at Biddle might quite easily be turned against those religious groups with whom Cromwell did sympathise: the Independents and Baptists. 'Where shall wee have men of a Universal Spirit?', he is reported to have asked when he heard of the City petition in favour of religious uniformity. 'Everyone desires to have liberty but none will give it.'[10] In his speech dissolving parliament on 22 January 1655 Cromwell berated MPs because they had not 'given a just liberty to Godly men of differing judgements', including

> many under the form of Baptism, who are sound in the Faith, only [they] may perhaps be different in judgement in some lesser matters . . . nothing will satisfy them, unless they can put their fingers upon their brethren's consciences, to pinch them there. . . . What greater hypocrisy than for those who were oppressed by

the Bishops to become the greatest oppressors themselves, so soon as their yoke was removed?[11]

What probably added to Cromwell's dismay at parliament's display of religious intolerance was further evidence
provided by the furore surrounding the Biddle case that
his vision of religious unity was receding. In a letter to an
old army friend, Lieutenant-Colonel Timothy Wilks, written
days before the dissolution, he was full of self-pity at the
criticisms hurled at him as he attempted to unite different
religious groups: 'whosoever labours to walk with an even
foot between the several interests of the people of God for
healing and accommodating their differences is sure to
have reproaches and anger from some of all sorts . . .
this is much of my position at the present, so unwilling are
men to be healed and atoned [i.e. at-oned, united]'.[12]
Equally distressing for Cromwell were the attacks made
in parliament on the army. He should not, however, have
been altogether surprised by these. Ever since the final
phase of the Civil War the army had been the target of
those who wanted an end to the high taxation necessary
for its upkeep and those who identified it with political revolution and the threat of social subversion. The last
months of 1654 witnessed a parliamentary attack on the
army, as hostile as the one mounted early in 1647 by Denzil
Holles and the political Presbyterians, which had sparked
off the politicisation of the New Model Army with such dramatic consequences. Late in September 1654 parliament
demanded a greater say in the choice of those councillors
responsible for the army when parliament was not in session, and this was followed in November and early December by a series of anti-army votes in support of this claim
and especially that after Cromwell's death the army be con-
trolled by the Council until parliament should meet and
then thereafter solely by parliament 'as they shall think fit'.
Ominous too (echoing the parliamentary measures of
April–May 1647) were demands for a reduction of the
monthly assessment used for the army's upkeep from
£90,000 to £30,000 and calls for a savage reduction in the
size of the army establishment and its replacement by local
militias. Cromwell and the Council made some efforts to
take the sting out of this attack by agreeing to reduce the

monthly assessment to £60,000, but they could not concede control of the army to parliament without ensuring the collapse of the godly cause. In his dissolution speech Cromwell made the point very clearly:

> If it [control of the army] should be yielded up at such a time as this, when there is as much need to keep this cause by it (which is most evident, at this time, impugned by all the enemies of it) as there was to get it, what would become of all? . . . It determines his [the Protector's] power, either for doing the good he aught, or hindering Parliaments from perpetuating themselves, or from imposing what religions they please on the consciences of men, or what government they please upon the nation. . . .[13]

It is possible to exaggerate Cromwell's political isolation by January 1655. Despite his lack of support in parliament, not all MPs were swept along by a desire for revenge upon the army, as can be seen by the size of the votes against parliament's attacks on the army. Yet the majority of MPs were anti-army, and Cromwell's failure to get conservative support for the regime is epitomised by the defection from his council of Anthony Ashley Cooper (the future earl of Shaftesbury), perhaps because Cromwell opposed suggestions that he should agree that the succession to the Protectorate should pass by hereditary right and not by election, as had been determined by the Instrument of Government. Moreover, not only were there parliamentary attacks on religious liberty of conscience, but there were also signs – notably 'the three colonels' petition' drafted by Colonels Matthew Alured, Thomas Saunders and John Okey in October 1654, and unrest in the army in Scotland and Yorkshire in December – that some soldiers shared the Commonwealthsmen's concern at the power given to the Protector by the Instrument of Government. Moreover, in the winter of 1654–55 Cromwell was beset by personal troubles. For much of October he was incapacitated after a serious riding accident in Hyde Park, when a pistol went off in his pocket after he fell from his horse, and he had to take to his bed for three weeks. (Even after that for a while his habitual walks in St James's Park were replaced by outings in a sedan chair.) Shortly afterwards his mother died, on

16 November, the climax of a miserable couple of months. Yet too much should not be made of the public political importance of these private personal events. Undoubtedly it was primarily political considerations that drove him to dissolve parliament precipitately on 22 January 1655. As he saw it, parliament, as in 1648 and 1653, had thrown away 'precious opportunities' to fulfill the godly cause.

Yet, also as in 1648 and 1653, Cromwell's impetuous political intervention is not solely explicable in terms of cool political calculation. As before, Cromwell's belief in providence played its part. When he recounted his political difficulties to Lieutenant-Colonel Wilks, about a week beforehand, he wrote:

> . . . the Lord will not let it always be so. If I have innocency and integrity the Lord hath mercy and truth and will own it. If in these things I have made myself my aim, and designed to bring affairs to this issue for myself, the Lord is engaged to disown me; but if the work be the Lord's . . . He will make His own councils stand; and therefore let men take heed lest they be found fighters against him.[14]

As will be seen, Cromwell was soon to worry that God did perhaps feel he was making 'myself my aim' (i.e. that his prime aim was his own self-advancement); but as yet he had none. 'I bless God I have been inured to difficulties', he told MPs when dissolving parliament on 22 January 1655, 'and I never found God wanting when I trusted in him. I can laugh and sing in my heart when I speak of these things to you.'[15] It is likely that he dismissed parliament in 1655 in an impulsive mood of providential, millenarian optimism, not unlike that which had led him to support both the execution of the king in January 1649 and the use of the army against the Rump Parliament in April 1653.

. . .

PERSONAL RULE: THE WESTERN DESIGN AND THE MAJOR – GENERALS

However, although there are many striking similarities between Cromwell's behaviour in January 1655 and earlier episodes in which periods of introspection and indecision culminated in sudden, impulsive action, Cromwell's reactions to what had happened in January 1655 differed in one respect from his attitudes in the aftermath of earlier crises. The main difference is that whereas before Cromwell had tried to return very quickly to policies of conciliation and constitutional respectability, in January 1655 he did not do so, and indeed it was to be a long time before he recovered his appetite for 'healing and settling'. Although Cromwell's desire for a constitutional settlement sanctioned by parliament was not totally extinguished, it is essential to an understanding of Cromwell's activities in the middle period of his Protectorate to recognise that his authoritarianism became more dominant than at any other time in his life.

Why this should have been is one of the most intriguing problems of Cromwell's political career. In part, though, the explanation is fairly straightforward in that it was now more difficult than ever for him to get wide political support for the godly cause. The number of his political enemies was greater than ever, swollen by those who had once been his friends: Lilburne and the Levellers, Saye and Sele and the powerful Political Independents, Harrison and the Fifth Monarchy Men, and now Haselrig, Scot and the republican MPs. The bitter experience of the recent parliament, moreover, must have led him to seek the pursuit of his aims by non-parliamentary means. Significantly, only three weeks after the dissolution, on 15 February 1655, he issued a proclamation on religion, which S.R. Gardiner called 'the charter of religious freedom under the Protectorate',[16] attempting to proceed with reformation by Protectoral decree. Moreover, during the next few months in 1655 and 1656 the dominant characteristic of his rule came to be a ruthless lack of compunction in dealing with those who questioned the constitutional validity of his rule and a determination to achieve his aims regardless of legal and constitutional niceties. At the Putney Debates in 1647 he had indulged in a rare piece of political theorising, declaring that force was only justified in the last resort 'in cases where we cannot get what is for the good of the kingdom without force'. In the months after the dissolution of the first protectorate parliament he seems to have decided that this was now the case. There are occasions when 'the Supreme Magistrate' should not be 'tied up to the ordinary rules', he said in a Declaration published on 31 October 1655,[17] and in September 1656 he even took this line of authoritarian reasoning to the extreme of saying that 'if nothing should be done but what is according to law, the throat of the nation may be cut, till we send for some to make a law'.[18]

However, what may also have pushed Cromwell towards authoritarian action, in addition to the fact that the parliamentary route was (at least temporarily) closed, is that in 1655 he did believe that the 'throat of the nation' was in danger of being cut. Early in the year government agents reported increased signs of activity among Royalists plotting against the regime. It is fairly easy now for historians, following the work of David Underdown, to poke fun at the amateurish, incompetent plans of groups of Royalist emigrés on the Continent, like the Sealed Knot (founded in 1653), aimed at organising a rebellion with disaffected elements in England, like the Political Presbyterians, soldiers and Levellers. It is now possible to see how unwilling were powerful English landed gentlemen to give military support to Royalist plotters. However, hindsight often gives historians false wisdom and it may be that this is a case in point. Cromwell and his councillors, without the benefit of hindsight, probably feared the worst. What is certain is that a planned nationwide Royalist uprising early in 1655 was a feeble, damp squib and only became of any significance in Wiltshire in March, when Royalist forces appeared led by John Penruddock. Penruddock's Rising was easily suppressed by government troops led by John Desborough, who was appointed 'major-general of the west' for this purpose. Most of the other plots never got beyond the planning stage, and the details of these were known to the government, largely through the agents employed by John Thurloe, who established himself, not only as the Protector's principal secretary, but also as the intelligence-gatherer *par excellence* of the Protectorate. On 16 March 1655, at the height of the Penruddock crisis, he felt confident enough to write that 'so far are they mistaken who dream that the affections of the people are towards the House of Stuart'.[19] It would be unwise to minimise the danger that Cromwell and the councillors felt the regime faced from the Royalist threat, but they had much information at hand to indicate its major limitations.

Therefore, as before at the great crisis points of Cromwell's political career, although 'rational' political considerations are important in explaining his actions, they do not provide a complete explanation. As before, in 1648–49 and 1653, so in 1655–56 Cromwell was driven by 'providence' as well as by 'necessity'. As has been seen, Cromwell's belief in providence had been greatly strengthened by great military victories in the 1640s and on campaigns in Ireland and Scotland. When he returned from the battlefield to the complex world of Westminster politics, however, Cromwell often found it harder to discern the dictates of providence, and he was beset by the nagging doubt that commonly troubled the godly that he might not after all have God's blessing. There are hints of desperation in the way he seized on events early in 1655 to convince himself that this was not so. On 24 March 1655 he interpreted the defeat of Penruddock's pathetic army as a sign of 'the hand of God going along with us' and this was mentally catalogued by him as another link in the 'chain of providences' that convinced him he had God's blessing.[20] Shortly afterwards, in a letter written on 25 March 1655, Cromwell heard of Blake's victory in the Mediterranean over the navy of the governor of Tunis, and he gratefully welcomed it as 'the good hand of God towards us in this action, who . . . was pleased to appear very signally with you'.[21]

Moreover, just over a month later, he heard about an event that had a major impact in bringing Cromwell's latent concern about providence to the fore and which convinced him that the godly cause was threatened abroad as well as at home and that decisive action was needed to counter it. Early in May 1655 news reached London of the massacre by the troops of their Catholic overlord, the duke of Savoy, of some 200–300 Protestants, known as the Vaudois or Waldensians, who lived in adjoining isolated Alpine valleys in Piedmont to the west of Turin. The impact on Cromwell and his co-religionists was one of horror, comparable, for example, to that felt by Elizabethan English Protestants when they heard of the St Bartholomew's Day massacre of French Protestant Huguenots by Catholic troops in Paris in 1572. Milton's sonnet calling for vengeance typifies the reaction of the godly in England in 1655 to the events in northern Italy:[22]

> Avenge, O Lord, thy slaugher'd saints, whose bones
> Lie scatter'd on the Alpine mountains cold;
> Ev'n them who kept Thy truth so pure of old,
> When all our fathers worshipp'd stocks and stones,
> Forget not; in Thy Book record their groans
> Who were Thy sheep, and in their ancient fold
> Slain by the bloody Piedmontese, that roll'd
> Mother with infant down the rocks. Their moans
> The vales redoubled to the hills, and they
> To Heav'n. Their martyr'd blood and ashes sow
> O'er all th' Italian fields, where still doth sway
> The triple Tyrant; that from these may grow
> A Hundredfold, who, having learn'd Thy way
> Early may fly the Babylonian woe.

Others, however, appealed not only to God but to Cromwell to act as the saviour of the Protestant cause. 'The whole Christendom have their eyes fixed on his Highness', wrote Jean-Baptist Strouppe, the minister of the French Protestant congregation in London, 'and all good men hope that he will avenge, or rather God will avenge, by his hand, such a hellish barbarousness . . . God has given him [a] great power to employ to his [God's] glory.'[23] Cromwell's letters to foreign states at this time reflect his sense of outrage at what had happened. At the end of May he and the Council set aside 14 June as a national day of fasting and humiliation, when public collections were to be made of money for the relief of the Vaudois Protestants. Cromwell himself gave £2,000, and £38,232 in all was raised.

What heightened the impact of these events on Cromwell was the close parallel between them and what had happened in Ireland in 1641. The report he received from Mr Leger, pastor at Geneva, in June 1655 could well have been a description made by Protestants of the Irish 'massacre' fourteen years earlier, and which (as has been seen) had had such a tremendous impact on Cromwell: 'Those massacrers have ripped the bellies of women with child and took the infants upon the points of their halberds and [that]

129

they have railed divers persons . . . to change their religion.'[24] Moreover, the connection between the two events was made explicit by those correspondents of Cromwell who reported the presence of Irish soldiers in the Duke of Savoy's army which had committed the atrocities. One of these wrote to reawaken in Cromwell (if that were necessary) the sense of peril and urgency that he had felt in 1641: 'Let the blood of Ireland be fresh in your view, and let their treachery cry aloud in your ears . . .'[25]

Cromwell's growing conviction that the godly cause was under attack in England and abroad, as well as the fact that the route to constitutional respectability was closed, helps to explain his lack of compunction in dealing with those who questioned the validity of his rule, which is a striking feature of the first months of 1655. Before the beginning of the major-generals experiment in the late summer a series of interrelated actions by the Protectorate Government illustrates this iron-fisted phase of Cromwellian rule. The first is the case of George Cony, which early in May came before the Court of Upper Bench (the name given in 1649 to the Court of King's Bench). Cony had been imprisoned in the previous November for refusing to pay customs duties on silk he had imported, and he had forcibly prevented customs officials from seizing his property, for which he was fined. When Cony refused to pay the fine he was imprisoned and his lawyers eventually based their case on his behalf on the grounds that the ordinances which authorised the levying of the customs duties were not valid, since they had not been approved by parliament, thus effectively attacking the Instrument of Government. The Council responded on 12 May by imprisoning Cony's lawyers for having the effrontery to question the protectoral prerogative, and they were only released when they retracted their case. Moreover, in a display of authoritarian power echoing Charles I's disregard for the law in the Five Knights' Case in 1627, the following week Lord Chief Justice Rolle was hauled before the Council for allowing the case to proceed, under which pressure he resigned. Already other senior judges had been harassed in a similar way to Rolle when they mounted a legal challenge to the Protectoral constitution. In April 1655 two judges were dismissed for having the temerity to question a treason ordinance issued by Protector and Council before parliament met in September 1654, and when two of the three commissioners of the great seal, Bulstrode Whitelocke and Thomas Widdrington, refused to execute the 1654 ordinance reforming the court of chancery, Protector and Council put the two men under great pressure for challenging the Instrument of Government, forcing their resignation on 6 June. Similarly, in July 1655 Sir Peter Wentworth, a republican Commonwealthsman from Warwickshire, was also called before the Council for refusing to pay taxes on the grounds that they were in contravention of the Instrument of Government and for persuading the sheriff of Coventry to arrest the local assessment commissioner. Wentworth, too, was bullied into withdrawing his opposition. What gives added force to these displays of Cromwellian high-handedness are the moves made in 1655 by Protectoral order in August and October to tighten the control of the press, not by enacting new measures but by appointing a three-man censorship committee to put existing regulations into effect and commanding that no one was to print 'books of news . . . unless authorised by us or our Council or licensed by those appointed thereto'.[26] Within a month of the first order all official and unofficial newsbooks were suppressed apart from *Mercurius Politicus* and *The Public Intelligencer*, which were Thursday and Monday editions of the government newspaper.

It would be neat – but wrong – to argue that the appointment of eleven major-generals in the late summer of 1655 to supervise the government of the English provinces is *wholly* explicable in terms of Cromwell's preference at this time for authoritarian methods aimed at imposing the godly reformation on the country by force. For one thing, Cromwell's motives for supporting the appointment of the major-generals were mixed. Even at the height of his authoritarian rule he was not unmindful of the need to get gentry support for his regime. In February he and the council reduced the total monthly assessment from £90,000 to £60,000, as parliament had demanded before it was dissolved. Moreover, the discussions in the Council, out of which came the major-generals experiment, began (in April and May) as an attempt to reduce the size of the standing army and to replace it with local militias, probably with at least one eye on the need to secure gentry support for the regime. Key positions were to be given to centrally appointed major-generals, godly men, to ensure that military control did not slip out of the hands of Cromwell and the Council, but the major-generals were to work with local commissioners. What further complicates the origins of the major-generals is that Cromwell was by no means the only person involved in their appointment. As has been seen, the influence of the Council on policy-making in the Protectorate is only now coming to be properly recognised, and Cromwell may have been justified when he later claimed that a major initiative for the appointment of major-generals came from military opinion in the Council, led by John Lambert. 'You thought it necessary to have Major-Generals', he told a meeting of army officers in February 1657.[27] Moreover, it is likely that Cromwell shared the concern for security even in the wake of the Penruddock fiasco. 'The sole end of this way of procedure', he said in a speech to the Lord Mayor and Corporation of London on 5 March 1657, 'was the security of the peace of the nation.'

But, significantly, he went on to add that 'the sole end' of the rule of the major-generals was also 'the suppression of vice and encouragement of virtue, the very end of magistracy'.[28] With all the above qualifications, it is difficult to escape the conclusion that Cromwell *primarily* considered the major-generals as agents for promoting the godly reformation, the task parliament had dismally failed, as he saw it, to undertake. What reinforces this conclusion is the way that the task given to the major-generals seems to have been shaped very much by the effect on Cromwell of news of another event overseas that influenced his outlook fundamentally at this time: the failure of the Western Design.

Like other aspects of Cromwellian policy, the Western Design originated in debates in the Protector's Council. In the summer of 1654 a rare record of those debates reveals conciliar opinion split on the advisability of making a major attack on Spanish possessions in the Caribbean. John Lambert was the spokesman of those who argued against it on economic grounds. Financing the occupation of Ireland and Scotland was alone hard enough, he argued; 'you must find more treasure; or else the West India designe must be lett fall'. But others countered this with the forecast that the cost would be balanced by the expenses already incurred in maintaining an unemployed navy – they had, said Cromwell, '160 ships swimming' already – and, above all, the expedition would bring 'great profitt' from the capture of Spanish ships and silver and by trade in Caribbean raw materials such as drugs, dyes and sugar. However, what swung the debate in favour of the Western Design were Cromwell's hopes that the expedition would yield more than material profits. 'Providence seemed to lead us hither', he is reported as having said in the debate; 'we consider this attempt, because wee thinke God has not brought us hither where wee are but to consider the worke that we may doe in the world as well as at home.'[29]

Just as Cromwell's aims as Protector at home – for liberty of conscience, for a 'reformation of manners', for rule by a single person and parliaments, and so on – were shaped decisively by the views that he had formed in association with political allies in the 1640s, so his attitudes to the Western Design owed much to ideas he had shared since at least the 1640s with Political Independents like Saye and Sele. Many of them had been investors in the Providence Island Company in the 1630s. In the Caribbean, the centre of Spanish influence in the New World, they had hoped to establish a godly colony that would bring them profit and strike a blow at Spain, the Antichrist. By 1641 that attempt had failed, as the Spanish overwhelmed the tiny colony at Providence. But, as Karen Kupperman has shown, the dream remained very much alive in the Political Independent circles in which Cromwell moved in the 1640s. It is not surprising, therefore, that Cromwell as Protector should be influenced by it. He wrote in October 1655 that 'we could all heartily wish that the island of Providence were in our hands again'. The conclusion of a printed Manifesto justifying the Western Design was not window-dressing but expressed one of its main purposes: to seize 'the noble opportunitie of promoting the glory of God and enlarging the bounds of Christ's Kingdom'.

A fleet of thirty ships left England for the Caribbean in December 1654, commanded by William Penn with Colonel Robert Venables in charge of an army of about 3,000 soldiers on board. Within six months of its departure it became clear that, in relation to Cromwell's high expectations, the Western Design was a complete flop. In contrast to the meticulous care which he put into his preparations for his own overseas expedition to Ireland in 1649, he allowed Venables and Penn to depart in December 1654 with ill-trained and ill-paid troops, with no clear instructions about which of the two commanders carried ultimate authority and (above all) with inadequate information about the strength of Spanish opposition in Hispaniola. Venables took his new wife with him to the Caribbean in the belief that the chief town on Hispaniola, San Domingo, 'not being considerably fortified would be possessed without much difficulty' and would soon become a British settlement, the beginning of making Cromwell's vision of a Protestant Caribbean a reality.[30] The expeditionary force left Barbados in March 1655 to attack Hispaniola and landed there on 14 April. Eleven days later it suffered a humiliating defeat at San Domingo and was forced to retreat towards the undefended island of Jamaica, which was eventually occupied after the loss of about half its men from disease. In the 1650s it was not foreseen that Jamaica would eventually in the eighteenth century become a sugar-producing colony and one of the major jewels in the British imperial crown, and its capture did nothing to soften the anger and humiliation felt in England at the expedition's failure. When Penn and Venables returned to England in the autumn they were questioned by the Council and then imprisoned in the Tower.

The effect on Cromwell was dramatic. When, on 24 July 1655, the news of the defeat at San Domingo two months previously finally reached him, he is said to have shut himself away alone in a room for a day. The reason is not hard to find: just as past military victories had been interpreted by him as signs of God's blessing, so he felt that the defeat of an expedition which he had intended as a means of exporting godly reformation into the heart of the antichristian empire of Spain must be a signal of God's rebuke. This interpretation of what had happened recurs in his letters in the summer and autumn of 1655. God 'hath very sorely chastened us', he wrote to Venables's successor in the Caribbean, Major-General Richard Fortescue, making arrangments for the settlement of Jamaica. 'We have cause to be humbled for the reproof God gave us at San Domingo, upon the account of our sins, as well as others.'[31] Similarly, to Penn's second-in-command in Jamaica, Vice-Admiral William Goodson, he recognised that 'the Lord hath greatly humbled us at that sad loss sustained at Hispaniola', and he drew the same conclusion that the cause of God's displeasure was that 'we have provoked the Lord and it is good for us to know so, and to be abased for the same . . . we should . . . lay our mouths . . . in the dust'.[32] Later during the kingship crisis, as will be seen, the doubt in Cromwell's mind was to haunt him, that it was his own sinfulness of self-pride and ambition that was the root cause of God's rebuke. But in 1655 Cromwell's references to the 'sins' were usually interpreted by him as those of the nation as a whole, not simply his own personal failings.

The principal effect of the Western Design débâcle on Cromwell, therefore, was to instil in him even more deeply than ever before a sense of urgency about the need for national reformation. Once again, as in past phases of doubts and crisis, it is striking how his mood of depression was tinged with hope, grounded in the belief that, as he wrote to Fleetwood on 22 June 1655, 'the will of the Lord will bring forth good in due time'.[33] His letters to his commanders and officials in the Caribbean in the autumn, too, reflect his conviction that 'though God has torn us yet he will heal us; though He hath smitten us, yet He will bind us up; after two days He will revive us, in the third day He will raise us up, and we shall live in His sight'.[34] But the essential requirement first, he told Fortescue in Jamaica, was that 'all manner of vice may be thoroughly discountenanced and severely punished; and that such a form of government may be exercised that virtue and godliness may receive due encouragement'.[35]

Cromwell in that letter was referring only to the need for reformation among the soldiers of the expeditionary force. However, the failure of the Western Design impelled him also towards national reformation. Even the first draft of the instructions to the major-generals on 22 August reflects his urgent desire 'to encourage and promote godliness and virtue and discourage all profaneness and ungodliness'. During the next few weeks a major debate took place in the Council about the brief to be given to the major-generals. Unfortunately the details of those debates are not known, but it is probable that the Council was split about what was the major-generals' principal function: the maintenance of security or the pursuit of moral reformation. There is little doubt that Cromwell had much sympathy with the group who argued for the latter. For Cromwell at least the lessons of the Western Design débâcle weighed heavily in persuading him to support the inclusion, in the final version of the instructions sent to the major-generals on 9 October, of new orders that emphasised that their task was the imposition of godly rule as well as the maintenance of security. It is no coincidence that five 'moral reform' orders were added to their instructions exactly when Cromwell was writing letters which blamed the Western Design's defeat on England's sinfulness and immorality which the additional instructions ordered the major-generals to combat. Already the instructions included a command that the major-generals should 'promote Godliness and Virtue' and execute 'the Laws against Drunkenness, Blasphemy, and taking of the Name of God in vain, by swearing and cursing, Plays and Interludes, and prophaning of the Lord's day, and such like wickedness and abominations'.[36] Now they were instructed also to control rigorously the number of alehouses and suppress gaming houses and brothels in London.

In many ways Cromwell's mood in 1655 resembles his feelings in 1648, that, not only should there be national reformation but also that the men guilty of stubbornly opposing this in the face of 'all the witnesses that God has borne' should be punished. In September Protector and Council decided that the new local militias should be financed by 'a decimation tax', the nickname given to a fine amounting to a 10 per cent charge on those with landed incomes of £100 p.a. and more, or with £1,500 in goods who had been supporters of the Royalist cause in the Civil War. The justifications given for this echo the language used in 1648 by Cromwell and others against the opponents of the army, including the king. On 31 October 1655 a protectoral declaration excused the decimation tax, on the grounds that Royalist delinquents were the cause of 'all our trouble and unsettlement' and the principal obstacles to the 'hopes we have conceived of seeing this poor nation settled and reformed from that spirit of profaneness which these men do keepe up and countenance'.[37] Moreover, an earlier declaration of 21 September 1655, which prohibited ex-Royalists from holding office, was justified on the grounds that they had shown that 'their end was, and still is (though in the utter ruin and desolation of these Nations) to set up that Power and Interest which Almighty God hath so eminently appeared against'.[38]

Cromwell's speech to his second Protectorate of 17 September 1656 denounced 'Papists and Cavaliers' (with rhetoric reminiscent of Macarthyite language used three centuries later against 'un-American' Communists in the United States) as 'un-Christian' and 'un-English-like'.[39]

Two more pieces of evidence contribute to a picture of a man whose millenarian passions were heightened and sustained in 1655–56 and whose providential mission remained strong. The first is the fact that the government regularly announced days of national humiliation in the mid-1650s in order to try to communicate Cromwell's mood to the people. For instance, 21 November 1655 was proclaimed a day of fasting and prayer to help bring about 'a settlement and reformation as hath been so long contended for, as has the weight of the work of this generation'. The second is Cromwell's interest in the winter of 1655–56 in the question of readmitting the Jews to England.

In November 1655 Cromwell agreed to the appointment of a conciliar committee of four men to consider the petition of Manessah ben Israel for permission for the Jews to live, trade and worship in England freely for the first time since the thirteenth century. The reasons why this was taken up by the republican Council are mixed. The economic benefits the Jews might bring the country were important. Major-General Edward Whalley wrote to Thurloe that 'doubtlesse, to say no more, they [the Jews] will bring in much wealth into the Common-wealth'. However, in the opinion of the most recent investigator of this episode, the economic argument was not the most important one in 1655. Nor was the notion of broad religious liberty: many councillors shared Cromwell's limited definition of liberty of conscience. The main reason why Cromwell persisted in supporting ben Israel's petition for the readmission of the Jews in discussions that continued in December 1655 is to be found in a widespread belief among godly Protestants that the conversion of the Jews was an essential precondition of the millenium. He was reported as saying that he 'had no ingagement to the Jews but what the Scriptures held forth; and since there was a Promise of their Conversion, means must be used to that end, which was the preaching of the Gospel'. Ben Israel's petition was blocked by the Council, but Cromwell lent his influence to the unofficial entry of the Jews to the country in the 1650s. What drove him to do this was the hope that one of the biblical prophecies about the conversion of the Jews would follow and take England one step nearer to the Promised Land.[40]

However, as might be expected, given the ambiguities of Cromwell's character and career up to this point, zealous as Cromwell was for reformation and ruthless as were some of the methods he adopted to achieve it in 1655–56, his moderate instincts for securing gentry support were never totally extinguished. Beneath the rhetoric in which he smeared Royalists as 'un-Christian and un-English-like' lay a Cromwell who often worked to protect some Royalist families from the worst effects of the decimation tax. In a typical instance in December 1655 Major-General Desborough reported that the decimation commissioners in the West Country had complained to him that Cromwell's favour towards Royalists was undermining their efforts to collect the tax. These and other instances of Cromwell's interventions on behalf of Royalists, at a time when he was also urging policies of vengeance against them, together with the reductions that were made in the size of the local militias in April 1656, are yet more examples of the ambiguities which characterised his career throughout his life .

But it would be dangerous to assume that Cromwell was already seeking ways to return to policies of conciliation and settlement in the summer of 1656, as has sometimes been suggested. Not only had he invested a lot of political capital in the major-generals but he continued to believe that they were having some success in bringing about the reformation he so badly wanted. In his opening speech to the second Protectorate parliament in September 1656 he said he believed that the major-generals experiment 'hath been very effectual towards the discountenancing of vice and settling religion, than anything else these fifty years'; and six months later, long after the experiment had been abandoned, he looked back on 'the excellent good service' done by the major-generals.[41] By the summer of 1656, however, war with Spain in the Caribbean had escalated into war with Spain in Europe as well, and (as English monarchical governments had found in the 1590s, 1620s and later 1630s) foreign wars were impossible to sustain without parliamentary financial support, even given the substantial increase in taxation available to mid-seventeenth-century governments since the financial reorganisation of the early 1640s. In late May/early June 1656 all the major-generals came to London to discuss with Protector and Council what was to be done to meet the financial crisis, and it was with some reluctance that Cromwell gave way to those who argued for a recall of parliament rather than for an increase in taxation by Protectoral decree. In July writs were issued for parliamentary elections to take place in August. That he agreed to this with some reluctance is an important clue to an understanding of the last phase of Cromwell's political career in which he remained as determined as ever to keep alive the goal of godly reformation.

.   .   .

NOTES AND REFEENCES

1. Abbot, vol. III, p. 184.
2. Abbott, vol. III, p. 587.
3. Abbott, vol. II, p. 579.
4. Abbott, vol. III, pp. 434, 442.
5. Abbott, vol. III, pp. 580, 593.
6. He used this phrase to describe his political role in a speech on 13 April 1657, Abbott, vol. IV, p. 470.
7. Abbott, vol. III, p. 581.
8. Abbott, vol. III, p. 449.
9. Abbott, vol. III, p. 834.
10. *Clark Papers*, vol. II, pp. xxxiv–xxxvii.
11. Abbott, vol. III, p. 586.
12. Abbott, vol. III, p. 572. Both S.R. Gardiner and C.H. Firth date this letter at the third week of January 1655.
13. Abbott, vol. III, p. 588.
14. Abbott, vol. III, p. 572.

15. Abbott, vol. III, p. 590.
16. S.R. Gardiner, *History of the Commonwealth and Protectorate 1649–46* (Windrush reprint, 1987, 4 vols), vol. III, p. 260.
17. Quoted in *ibid.*, vol. III, p. 329.
18. Abbott, vol. IV, p. 275.
19. Abbott, vol. III, p. 655.
20. Abbott, vol. III, p. 671.
21. Abbott, vol. III, p. 745.
22. Quoted in Gardiner, *Commonwealth*, vol. IV, p. 193.
23. Quoted in C.P. Korr, *Cromwell's New Model Foreign Policy: England's Policy Towards France 1649–58* (University of California Press, 1975), pp. 151–2.
24. *TSP*, vol. III, p. 460.
25. *TSP*, vol. III, p. 467.
26. Quoted by P.W. Thomas in his introduction to *The English Revolution: III. Newsbooks 5, vol. 1, Mercurius Politicus* (Cornmarket Press, 1971), p. 8 .
27. Abbott, vol. IV, p. 417.
28. Abbott, vol. IV, p. 112.
29. Abbott, vol. IV, pp. 377–8.
30. K. Kupperman, 'Errand to the Indies: Puritan colonisation from Providence Island through the Western Design', *William and Mary Quarterly*, 3rd series, vol. 45, 1988. Quoted in Gardiner, *Commonwealth*, vol. IV., p. 130.
31. Abbott, vol. III, pp. 857–8.
32. Abbott, vol. III, p. 859.
33. Abbott, vol. III, p. 756.
34. Abbott, vol. III, p. 860.
35. Abbott, vol. III, p. 858.
36. Abbott, vol. III, p. 845.
37. Gardiner, *Commonwealth*, vol. III, pp. 328–9.
38. Abbott, vol. III, p. 828.
39. Abbott, vol. IV, p. 264.
40. David S. Katz, *Philo-Semitism and the Readmission of the Jews to England 1603–55* (University of California Press 1982), p. 7; Abbott, vol. IV, p. 53.
41. Abbott, vol. IV, pp. 274, 494.

Chapter 7

THE CONTINUING QUEST FOR SETTLEMENT AND REFORMATION
(September 1656 – September 1658)

The last years of Oliver Cromwell's political career have often been depicted as a period of reaction as the Cromwellian regime drifted towards a monarchical-type constitution. From this standpoint, the Humble Petition and Advice has been seen as an essential step on the road that led to the restoration of the monarchy in 1660. Cromwell is sometimes portrayed in his later years as a man whose radical vitality finally ebbed away as he buckled under the strain of the long struggle to reconcile the irreconcilable: constitutional respectability and godly reformation. This, however, is a misleading interpretation of his last years. There is no doubt that at the end of 1656 he recovered his appetite for reaching a settlement through parliament, as he had tried to do on previous occasions, notably in the aftermath of the Civil War, the execution of the king, and the establishment of the Protectorate. The word 'settlement' recurs with great frequency in his letters and speeches in 1656–57, reaching a crescendo in the spring of 1657. 'You have need to look at settlement', he told a committee of MPs on 13 April 1657: 'I would rather I were in my grave than hinder you in anything that may be for settlement, for the nation needs it and never needed it more . . . .Whatsoever any man thinks, it equally concerns one man as another to go on to a settlement.'[1] When he saw the committee, eight days later, he pressed the same point:

I am hugely taken with the word Settlement, with the thing and with the notion of it. I think he is not worthy to live in England that is not. I will do my part as far as I am able to expel that man out of the nation,

141

that doth not affect of that in the general to come to a settlement . . . a nation . . . is like a house . . . it cannot stand without settlement.[2]

Moreover, in 1657 he concurred in the abandonment of the major-generals experiment and accepted a revised parliamentary constitution. Yet there is no doubt either that his commitment to the cause of reformation remained intact, and that he continued to put the godly cause before that of a parliamentary settlement, saying, on 3 April 1657: 'Civil liberty . . . ought to be subordinate to a more peculiar interest of God.'[3]

The first section of this chapter is concerned with the question of why in the first session of the second Protectorate parliament, from September 1656 to May 1657, Cromwell slowly returned to the attempt he had often made before to reconcile the two dominating concerns of his life. But it is also concerned with the question of why Cromwell, when his aim was to secure a parliamentary-approved constitutional settlement, rejected the offer of the crown made by a majority in parliament, instead of accepting it which would have sent his regime spinning merrily along the road to settlement.

The second part of his chapter deals with the reasons for the sudden collapse of Cromwell's last Protectorate parliament, early in 1658, and the failure of the constitution revised by the Humble Petition and Advice to provide the Protector with a co-operative parliament. It also raises the last major puzzle of Cromwell's political career: did the failure to secure a co-operative parliament, together with illnesses and personal tragedies in the last months of his life, extinguish the vitality and fire that had driven him on throughout his impetuous and tempestuous career?

. . .

KING OLIVER?

As in the summer of 1654, so Cromwell two years later made few preparations for the coming parliamentary session. His tendency to rely on providence was now reinforced by a lack of any enthusiasm to meet parliament, and it is not surprising to learn from the work of Peter Gaunt that Cromwell distanced himself from the exclusion from parliament of about a hundred MPs, which was carried out by the Council in the weeks following the parliamentary elections. (The aim of this was to gag the most vociferous opponents of the army and the Instrument of Government.) That Cromwell was hardly ecstatic about meeting parliament is also suggested by his speech at its opening on 17 September 1656. Like most of Cromwell's parliamentary speeches this one is not easy to analyse. Typically, it began with an intention to be brief, but not only did it become excessively long (perhaps taking two or three hours to deliver) but it is rambling and has no clear pattern. However, the speech did steer clear of the seductive 'healing and settling' theme that had characterised Cromwell's opening remarks to his first parliament in September 1654. It opened with a great tirade against the 'un-English-like' Papists and Royalists – 'the enemies within' – as well as the threat of Spanish invasion. Its first main aim was designed to shock MPs into providing the subsidies, which was the main reason why Cromwell and his Council had finally agreed to calling it in the summer. Its second main aim was to impress on MPs the urgency of reformation. The speech contains clear evidence of the powerful influence on Cromwell (which has been noted in chapter 5) of the Old Testament stories that illustrated the need of the Israelites to purge themselves of sin in order to get God's help to take them from Egyptian bondage out of the wilderness and into the promised land. Like the Israelites, Cromwell implied, the English needed to reform themselves. We do not want, he said,

> a captain to lead us back into Egypt, if there be such a place – I mean metaphorically and allegorically so – that is to say, returning to all those things that we think we have been fighting against . . . . I am confident, that the liberty and prosperity of this nation depends upon reformation . . . make it a shame to see men to be bold in sin and profaneness, and God will bless you. . . . Truly these things do respect the souls of men, and the spirits, which are the men. The mind is the man. If that be kept pure, a man signifies somewhat . . . .[4]

Cromwell left MPs in no doubt that they were expected to provide reformation as well as money, but typically his speech gave no specific guidance about what reforms were wanted, and lacked any real optimism that they would comply; instead it pessimistically concluded by warning them not to 'dispute of unnecessary and unprofitable things that may divert you from carrying on so glorious a work', as he considered they had done two years earlier.[5]

When parliament began its work, however, it proved to be exceedingly co-operative and productive. Surprisingly, the massive conciliar exclusion of over a hundred elected MPs provoked less critical comment at Westminster than outside parliament. The latter is typified by a pamphlet published later, *A Narrative of the Late Parliament*, which scathingly compared the exclusions (making the point Dorothy Osborne had made about the dissolution of the Rump in 1653) with Charles I's breach of parliamentary privileges on 4 January 1642 when he attempted to arrest the five members: was not the exclusion 'a crime twenty-fold beyond that of the late King's, in going to seclude the five members, so highly disresented in that day by the people, and afterwards attended with so great feud and bloodshed?'.[6] The only significant protest in parliament, by Sir George Booth, who on 8 September 1656 presented a petition signed by seventy-nine of the excluded MPs, led to a five-day debate which threatened to escalate into a major constitutional row against the misuse of protectoral power. But this did not materialise and MPs proved to be very co-operative during the next few weeks, passing acts against 'the pretended title of Charles Stuart' and declaring attacks on the Protector's person as treason. Moreover, although subsidies for the war against Spain were not passed until January 1657, MPs indicated strong support for the war. Parliament set aside 8 October 1656 as a day of public thanksgiving for the capture of a Spanish treasure fleet by the British navy on 9 September, and Cromwell predictably took pleasure from this as a providential sign. Not only was it 'a dispensation' and 'so suitable and seasonable a mercy' but it was an indication that God 'will still appear as a present help in our time of need'.[7] No doubt the word 'still' indicated Cromwell's relief that here was a reassuring token that, despite recent 'rebukes', he and the nation still had God's blessing.

What was also welcome to Cromwell was parliament's

willingness to press ahead with measures of reform. Before the end of the year proposals were being proceeded with, among other things, to regulate alehouses, set the poor to work, and put an end to 'undecent fashions' among women, which were all matters dear to the heart of the the godly and their concern for the 'reformation of manners'. Even Cromwell's hopes for legal reform were met early in November, when Lambert's proposals for a court of law and equity at York were taken up by MPs and plans were discussed to establish regional registry offices for proving wills and for county land registries. When Cromwell addressed the House for a second time on 27 November, he enthused at what MPs had achieved: 'though you have sat but a little time . . . you have made many good laws, the effect whereof the people of the Commonwealth will with comfort find hereafter'.[8]

Not surprisingly, though, hatred of the army (and of the Instrument of Government which many MPs considered to be a military constitution) and strong religious intolerance – the issues which had caused major clashes between the Protector and his first parliament – soon reappeared in the second parliament. On 28 October 1656 an Irish MP William Jephson, raised the question of converting the Protectorate to an hereditary one, and although it got no significant support in parliament, the reports of foreign ambassadors suggest that the question of revising the constitution in order to weaken the influence of the army was discussed privately, and that some men close to Cromwell were heavily involved. As so often with the 1650s, there is not enough source material for a full analysis of the way decisons were reached during the Protectorate. Yet there are enough indications to make clear that it was not simply the rule of one man. Not only was the role of the Council written into the first Protectorate constitution, the Instrument of Government, forcing Cromwell to take account of its recommendations, but also Cromwell's actions throughout his life were influenced by the views of those around him. It is instructive, therefore, to see that in the winter of 1656–57 conservative, civilian politicians appear often to have been among those he looked to for advice. In February 1657 there was even a report that Oliver St John and Pierrepoint had been at Whitehall, but his contacts with Political Independent allies of the 1640s were now rare. More significant at the end of 1656 was his close association with a group of advisers who had no connections with the army: Edward Montague, Charles Howard, Sir Charles Wolseley, Viscount Fauconberg (soon to be his son-in-law), Nathaniel Fiennes, Bulstrode Whitelocke, Sir Thomas Widdrington and (above all) Robert Boyle, Lord Broghill, who (for a brief time in 1656–57) was Cromwell's main political confidant in a way that at various times in the past Ireton, Lambert, Harrison, St John and others had been. Cromwell's association with Broghill had begun in 1649 when he persuaded Broghill to join him on his Irish expedition. Like his father, Robert, first earl of Cork, who had made a fortune as a settler and planter in Ireland, Broghill had worked for the protestantisation of Ireland, but in opposing the Irish rebellion in the 1640s he had fought with the Royalist army in Ireland under the earl of Ormonde. After helping Cromwell secure English rule in Ireland, his main political aim in British (Scottish, as well as English) politics in the 1650s was to push the regime towards a monarchical, 'civilian' constitution, stripped of any military influence. Broghill and his friends thought in December 1656 that 'now is the time of doing somewhat to purpose, the designes of the M[ajor] Generalls beeing now become visibly dangerous, and especially his Highness having so complyant and well affected Parliament to back him therein, and the sober people beeing withall generally big with hopes of seeing that good day of settlement'.

Before the end of 1656, however, there is not one shred of evidence that Cromwell himself gave his support to any such move. He was even as unwilling to consider the question of the succession as had been Elizabeth I. Yet in the early weeks of the new year Cromwell's attitude changed and by the end of February he was openly championing the abandonment of the Instrument of Government in favour of a parliamentary-approved constitution. On 27 February, with considerable political bravery, he declared to an audience of army officers who were deeply opposed to change: 'It is the time to come to a settlement and lay aside arbitrary proceedings, so unacceptable to the nation.'[9]

Why did Cromwell's attitude change? The co-operative

manner of parliament in the first few months of session may have influenced him somewhat, as did, undoubtedly the arguments of those like Broghill who emphasised the political support the regime would gain. But the most important reason was the Nayler case, which became a notorious *cause célèbre* in the winter of 1656 and had many important repercussions on the politics of the last period of the Protectorate. The 'crime' for which James Nayler (an ex-soldier in Lambert's northern army, who in the 1650s became an Independent preacher and then a Quaker evangelist) was indicted, found guilty, and eventually savagely punished, was that in October 1656, as part of a revivalist evangelical tour of the West Country, he had entered Bristol, riding an ass and acclaimed by his supporters, re-enacting Christ's entry into Jerusalem. He was subsequently arrested by local magistrates and brought to London to face the charge in parliament in November and December of 'horrid blasphemy'. In the light of the resurgence of religious fundamentalism in late twentieth-century Britain what happened next seems less surprising to modern eyes than it once did. Those MPs who tried to argue that Nayler was not guilty and that parliament had, in any case, no right under the Instrument of Government to try him were howled down. 'Let us all stop our ears and stone him', said one member,[10] and the House voted on 8 December without a division that Nayler was guilty of 'horrid blasphemy'. After a protracted debate Nayler was sentenced to be branded, bored through the tongue, flogged twice and then imprisoned for life.

What lay behind this display of religious bigotry, anger and savagery was the fact that the Quakers had become by the mid-1650s the focus of the fears of the wealthy and propertied about what might be the consequences of relaxing the penal laws compelling religious uniformity. Quakers were, after the Baptists, the most numerous identifiable unorthodox religious Protestant group – by 1650 there were about 50,000. They were centred largely in northern England, but through the work of evangelists like Nayler Quaker ideas were being spread throughout the country. Of all the religious groups that emerged in the 1650s the Quakers developed most fully the Protestant concept of 'the inner light' – that men and women should follow their own consciences rather that the dictates of churches and ministers – and their enemies feared, with some justice, that some Quakers interpreted this, not only as a licence for sexual permissiveness, but also for attacks on the existing social order. Quakers refused to pay tithes or to take off their hats in the presence of those considered by others to be their social superiors, and, in great contrast to their meek, peace-loving successors from the later seventeenth century onwards, were not against taking militant action, violently interrupting church services with which they disagreed.

Cromwell had no sympathy whatsoever for views like these and would have agreed with Major-General Skippon, who said in the parliamentary debate on the Nayler case that 'if this [allowing Nayler to act as he did] be liberty, God deliver me from such liberty'.[11] Indeed Cromwell made it clear himself when writing to the Speaker of parliament, Sir Thomas Widdrington, on 25 December 1656 that 'we [here Cromwell used that word in its singular, royal sense] detest and abhor the giving or occasioning the least countenance to persons of such opinions and practices, or who are under the guilt of such crimes as are commonly reputed to [James Nayler]'.[12] As has been seen Cromwell's definition of religious liberty did not extend to those who acted and spoke as outrageously as did the Quakers. But that was the extent of Cromwell's agreement with those MPs who had howled for Nayler to be punished. What worried him deeply about what had happened was that, like the Biddle case earlier, this was yet another indication of the alarming discrepancy between himself and opinion represented in parliament about the extent of religious liberty that could reasonably be allowed. Cromwell no more approved of Naylor's views than he did of Biddle's, but what frightened him about the parliamentary reactions to both men were the disturbing indications than many MPs (unlike him) drew no distinction between extremist Socinians or Unitarians, like Biddle, or Quakers, like Nayler, and those moderate groups like Baptists and Independents that Cromwell was willing and anxious to tolerate. This was the point he put forcibly to the meeting of army officers he addressed on 27 February 1657. Might not (he asked them), if nothing were done to check parliament's religious intolerance, 'the Case of James Nayler . . . happen to be your own case? '

This, however, was a fear that was not new; indeed Cromwell had lived with it since at least 1644, when his quarrel with the earl of Manchester had brought home to him the possible implications of Presbyterian intolerance. What was new about the Nayler case was Cromwell's reaction to it, in that he saw constitutional change as a means of checking parliamentary intolerance. He asked in his letter to the Speaker on 25 December 1656 by what right they had proceeded against Nayler, raising by implication the constitutional ambiguities of the Instrument of Government; and in his speech to army officers on 27 February 1657 he explicitly explained that the constitutional lesson of the Nayler case was that 'they [the single-chamber parliament] stood in need of a check or balancing power (meaning the House of Lords or a House so constituted)'.[13]

Before that meeting, however, Cromwell had already given clear signals that he was ready to abandon the authoritarian strategies of 1655–56. When a Militia Bill for continuing the decimation tax was discussed in parliament on 7 January 1757 his son-in-law, John Claypole, opposed it, in all probability with the Protector's connivance, thus effectively ending the major-generals experiment. Moreover, when on 23 February 1657 Sir Christopher Packe introduced a paper outlining a new constitution – the embryo of the Humble Petition and Advice – it was widely believed at the time that he acted as the agent for powerful 'civilian' interests among the Protector's advisers, notably Broghill, Whitelocke and Wolseley, who in a time-honoured fashion pioneered by Elizabethan privy councillors were using the Commons as a vehicle to press policies they had been advocating at court against Cromwell's 'military' advisers, Desborough, Fleetwood and especially Lambert, whose brainchild the Instrument of Government was. Moreover, it was a tactic that worked. As has been seen, Cromwell spoke enthusiastically for constitutional change to army officers only four days after Packe's proposals were first floated, and when the Humble Petition and Advice was presented to him in its polished form on 31 March after a month of parliamentary debates on its provisions, he gave it a generous welcome then and in the days following: it provided for 'the settlement of the chiefest things that can fall the hearts of men to desire', he said in a speech in the Banqueting Hall on 8 April. 'You have provided for the liberty of the people of God and of the nation', he praised a parliamentary committee on 21 April, 'and I say, he sings sweetly that sings a song of reconciliation betwixt these two interests . . . I think in this government [constitution] you have made them consist'.[14]

Given Cromwell's political roots in the Political Independency of the 1640s and his more recent experiences of single-chamber parliaments, his welcome for the constitutional clauses of the Humble Petition and Advice is not surprising. Its provisions for a limited, hereditary monarchy, for parliamentary approval of the great officers of state and for parliamentary approval of taxation echo those of *The Heads of the Proposals*. Moreover, the establishment of a second chamber – 'the Other House' – whose members were to be nominated by Protector and Council was not unwelcome to a man who had sought to prevent the abolition of the House of Lords in 1649. Above all, the second chamber would provide the protection for Cromwell's co-religionists against the excessive religious intolerance which had been released by the Nayler case. 'It will be', wrote Thurloe, ' a great security and bulwark to the honest interest.'[15] Cromwell's welcome for the religious clauses of the Humble Petition does not seem as surprising as it once did, now that it is apparent that he never aimed at unlimited religious freedom for *all* Protestants. The limitation put on religious freedom by the new constitution – that 'liberty be not extended to Popery or Prelacy, or to the countenancing such who publish horrid blasphemies, or practice to hold forth licentiousness or profaneness under the profession of Christ'[16] – was one that accorded with the views often voiced by Cromwell as Protector. His praise for MPs in the Humble Petition and Advice as regards 'the Liberty of men professing Godliness under a variety of forms amongst us, you have done that which was never done before' was lavish but not insincere.[17]

Although there were things about the Humble Petition and Advice that worried Cromwell – such as the financial provision of £1,300,000 p.a. which fell (Cromwell reckoned) £600,000 p.a. short of what was needed – the main stumbling block in the way of Cromwell's acceptance of it was the offer it made to him of the crown. There is no doubt that this is why Cromwell spent five weeks agonising over the proposed constitution, stretching near to breaking point the patience of MPs and councillors anxious for his answer. On 14 and 15 April he did not keep appointments to meet a parliamentary committee on the proposed constitution, saying he was ill. Later he became more inventive and more rude in his excuses; on 7 May he postponed two more meetings with MPs, saying he had to inspect a horse that had been given him. On other occasions Cromwell tried to make light of the decision facing him. According to Ludlow, during the kingship crisis he dined with Desborough and Fleetwood and adopted a tactic he had used in discussions with army officers on the same subject nearly ten years before, early in 1648: 'he began to droll with them about monarchy, and speaking slightly of it, said it was but a feather in a man's cap'.[18] But animated moments like this (even if they occurred) were exceptional during these weeks. More typical of Cromwell's mood are the comments made by someone closer to the Protector than Ludlow at this time. Thurloe on two occasions in April told correspondents about Cromwell's 'great difficulties in his own mind' and how he 'keeps himself reserved from everybody that I know of'.[19] Moreover, on the rare occasions when he did appear in public, as he did when meeting a parliamentary deputation on 16 April, the image of Cromwell is of a man under great mental stress: 'he came out of his chamber [according to a newspaper report] half unready in his gown, with a black scarf round his neck', obviously torn apart by indecision.[20]

Why did Cromwell agonise over the offer of the kingship and why did he eventually (on 8 May) turn it down? It is difficult to believe, given his successful bravado confrontation with army officers on 27 February, that fear of the army's reaction was a major consideration. At moments of crisis in the past he had had no difficulty in crushing army discontent. Probably the main political consideration that told against accepting the crown was his calculation that as King Oliver he would find it harder than ever to resist the influence of those like Broghill who were hostile to godly reformation. Yet as has been seen, Cromwell's political decisions can rarely be fully understood without reference to his belief in providence and his attempts to discern what providence dictated he should do. Throughout his public life, certainly from the mid-1640s, Cromwell was never short of advice from the godly inside and outside the army on this matter, like William Bradford's letter to him on 4 March 1657 with its nostalgic references to the heady days of war when the dictates of providence were clear to Cromwell: 'I am of that number, my Lord, that still loves you, and greatly desires to do so, I having gone along with you from Edgehill to Dunbar. The experiences that you have had of the power of God at these two Places, and betwixt them, methinks, should often make you shrink, and be at a stand in, this thwarting, threatened change.'[21] What made Cromwell especially susceptible to sentiments like these at this time was that he had just been given cause by the failure of the Western Design to doubt whether he was 'the apple of God's eye'. What would God think if he restored the monarchy which had been abolished with God's blessing in 1649? Would that not be interpreted as the sin of pride, ambition and self-advancement? It is important to stress that this was a thought he voiced immediately he was given the Humble Petition and Advice on 31 March. 'If these considerations [the powers detailed in the new constitution] fall upon a person or persons that God has no pleasure in, that perhaps may be the end of this work', he told MPs as he received the proposed new constitution.[22] On 13 April he expanded on the providential reasons against accepting the title of king:

> Truly the providence of God has laid this title aside providentially . . . God has seemed providentially not only to strike at the family but at the name . . . God . . . hath not only dealt so with the persons and the family, but he hath blasted the title . . . I would not seek to set up that that providence hath destroyed and laid in the dust, and I would not build Jericho again.[23]

Accepting the crown would have helped increase the support for his regime, but the deciding argument against acceptance for Cromwell was the possibility that God, like those godly men, including John Owen, who urged its rejection, would interpret its acceptance as a sign that Cromwell had opted for worldly advancement in favour of godly reformation. As at other times in his career whenever Cromwell feared that the cause espoused by parliament endangered the godly cause, he was torn by indecision but eventually decided to protect the latter.

Parliament had earlier told him that he must accept all elements of the new constitution or the constitutional proposals would be withdrawn. Nevertheless, on 25 May, two weeks after he rejected the crown, he was offered an amended version of the Humble Petition and Advice, by which he was to retain the title of Protector. A month later on 26 June he was re-invested as Lord Protector with great pomp. Unlike the drab occasion when he had been installed as Protector in December 1653, the ceremony in the Painted Chamber in Whitehall in June 1657 was regal in its splendour. Cromwell entered the chamber wearing an ermine-lined robe in a procession that included the Lord Mayor and aldermen of London, members of the Commons and the French and Dutch ambassadors, and he then took the oath of office as Protector after being given the sword of state and a sceptre of gold. This, together with his subsequent actions has sometimes been interpreted as a marked shift towards monarchical ways. As has been seen, His Highness Oliver Cromwell's daughters, Frances and Mary, married peers in November, and he created two hereditary peers. Moreover, in July Cromwell forced John Lambert, his senior general, to resign his commission as major-general after Lambert refused to swear an oath of allegiance to him as required by the new parliamentary constitution. Lambert withdrew (for a second time and again temporarily) from the army and from politics. In ousting a man who had seemed and probably thought himself the most obvious military successor to him as Protector, Cromwell apparently seemed to be signalling the shift of his regime towards a traditional civilian settlement of the sort advocated by Broghill. Yet 'apparently' is the key word. Certainly that is not how Cromwell's rejection of the crown and re-investiture as Protector was interpreted at the time. When Cromwell turned down the crown 'civilian' Cromwellians like Broghill withdrew (temporarily) in disgust. They knew (as should historians) that the real significance of his rejection of the crown was that he had signalled that he was not willing to allow his drive towards reformation to be shackled by constitutional chains.

. . .

A BROKEN MAN?

The last year of Cromwell's political career was dominated by the ending of the second session of the second Protectorate parliament, which (unlike the first session) lasted less than three weeks and was ended by a display of Cromwellian impetuousity and anger akin to that with which Cromwell had dissolved parliaments in April 1653 and January 1655. The reason why MPs in the second session of parliament were much less co-operative than in the first are not hard to identify. The invitations Cromwell sent to his former Political Independent friends, especially Wharton and Saye and Sele, to sit in the Other House were ignored. Cromwell therefore was forced to appoint to it those who would have provided him with invaluable support in the Commons, as they had done in the first session. Of the sixty-three men nominated by Cromwell to sit in the Other House about thirty were MPs who had given him consistent support in the Commons in the first session. Moreover, the hundred or so excluded MPs of 1656 were again allowed to take their seats when parliament reconvened in January 1658 and these included experienced MPs such as Haselrig and Scot, whose hatred of the Protector was not in any way assuaged by his acceptance of a parliamentary constitution. Furthermore, to past grievances they felt at 'military absolutism' was now added the affront of a second chamber that looked suspiciously like a House of Lords. The republican MPs devoted the brief weeks of the session to a single-minded and uncompromising attack on the bicameral nature of the new constitution, upholding the republican virtues of a constitution in which a unicameral parliament held sole executive and legislative power as the Rump had done after 1649.

That attack should have been – and surely was – expected by Cromwell. On 25 January he lectured MPs for not combatting 'the calamities and divisions amongst us', following a format that had become by now familiar in his speeches to parliaments.[24] What he did not perhaps expect, and what caused him to dissolve parliament suddenly, just over a week later, was the support the Commonwealths-men received from elements in the army. In the last days of January 1658 a republican-inspired petition circulated in the City, demanding the abolition of the Protectorate and the Other House and the restoration of a single-chamber parliament with all the powers possessed by the Rump in the early 1650s. It also demanded religious liberty and that officers should not be dismissed except by court martial, and there were disturbing signs that the petition was sup-ported by some soldiers. On 4 February, the day the peti-tion was to be presented to the Commons, Cromwell, acting alone (none of his immediate advisers including Thurloe appear to have known of his intentions) rushed to the House and after an angry speech he dismissed his last parliament in order to prevent the growth of army disunity.

The last months of Cromwell's life are scantily recorded, thus leaving ample room for varying interpretations of them. The most common one is that after the end of his last parliament the Protector degenerated to become a deep-ly depressed and pathetic figure, so that, according to one recent account, 'as the summer drew on, it became obvious that the disappointment of the spring had not just stunned Cromwell, it had broken him'.[25] It is far easier to agree with the proposition that Cromwell's last months were filled with disappointment than that he died a 'broken' man. He must have been distressed that the political and personal problems he faced in his last months were as daunting as any he had ever faced before. Moreover, there was much about the country he ruled that fell short of his expectations and hopes. Yet his achievements as Protector were considerable and obvious enough to provide some consolation for any disappointment he may have felt. It is far from certain that Cromwell's burning reforming auth-oritarian enthusiasm to give 'the people what's good for them' had been extinguished before he died on 3 Septem-ber 1658.

There is no doubt that the problems he faced after the dissolution of parliament in February were very severe. His government's financial situation went from bad to worse, as government expenditure escalated on an expensive foreign policy, including the cost of garrisoning Scotland and Ire-land. Government income fell as the monthly assessment tax was periodically cut to curry favour with the propertied classes. The Humble Petition and Advice reduced the tax from £60,000 to £35,000 per month. Cromwell and the Council were therefore forced to embark on expedients like authorising free quarter for its troops and going cap in hand, like Stuart monarchs before and later, to City merchants for loans. It soon became apparent that the only realistic way out of the financial crisis was to call another parliament to authorise the raising of taxation levels and with that prospect, of course, loomed the awesome possibility of renewed parliamentary opposition and pressure on him to take the crown.

What made these problems more daunting than ever is that Cromwell must have been hard hit by the breach that occurred in the days following the dissolution with military comrades who had fought with him since the beginning of the Civil War. One by one, during the 1650s, former allies and friends had left his side, and the latest to do so were six officers whom he cashiered on 11 February after they refused to withdraw their view that the Cromwellian Protectorate had departed from the Good Old Cause. It must have been especially hurtful that one of them was Captain William Packer, the commander of his own regiment of horse, and that all six were Baptists. It is stretching the evidence too far to suggest that this brought on 'an acute psychological crisis',[26] but Cromwell's conscience was always vulnerable to accusations from those he considered like himself 'God's children'. Moreover, as so often before, with the political crisis came an attack of ill-health. Late in February he was reported to be sick in bed with 'a very dangerous impostume in his back'. At the same time his new son-in-law, Robert Rich, died and soon after that his favourite daughter, Elizabeth Claypole, fell seriously ill with cancer, which killed her on 6 August.

There is little room to doubt that the strain on him of these political and personal problems 'drank up his spirit' (as his steward, John Maidstone, later said). Cromwell himself in February remarked that he had carried 'a burden upon my back for the space of fifteen or sixteen years. . . I would have been glad, as to my own conscience and spirit, to have been living under a wood-side, to have kept a flock of sheep, rather than to have undertaken such a place as this was.'[27] What is doubtful, however, is whether all this meant that Cromwell now surrendered to depression and torpor in his last months and that he died a broken man who had lost the will to live. This is a view that does not take account of the extraordinary amount of time that Cromwell, as will be seen, continued to devote to foreign affairs. Nor was he inactive in dealing with internal problems. He can be criticised for the fact that he dealt with the problem of who was to succeed him far too late, but it is highly probable that by the end of 1657 he had made up his mind who his successor was to be and before he died he left instructions to Thurloe and his councillors accordingly. Under the Humble Petition and Advice Cromwell was empowered to name his successor and George Bate, his doctor in 1658, later alleged that Cromwell had nominated Fleetwood soon after his second installation as Protector. But, if he did so, it is highly likely that he changed his mind by November or December 1657. Although he liked Fleetwood, who was married to his daughter Bridget, he was scathing about Fleetwood's political abilities. In February he called him 'a milk-sop' when Fleetwood advised caution as Cromwell was about to dissolve parliament. Before that, in November 1657 Cromwell replaced Fleetwood as Lord Deputy of Ireland by his younger son, Henry Cromwell, and soon after he brought his elder son, Richard, from his estates in Hampshire to be groomed for the succession. And in September Richard succeeded his father with no hint of opposition.

Nor was there anything slack about the ruthless way the Cromwellian regime dealt with Royalist plotters in the spring and early summer of 1658. A High Court of Justice, appointed in April, met from the end of May to try men caught in Thurloe's intelligence spy net, including John Hewett, John Lord Mordaunt and Henry Slingsby. Only Mordaunt escaped. Others went to the gallows. John Lisle, the president of the High Court, was reported by *Mercurius Politicus* to have sent Slingsby to his death with the comment that Slingsby's crime was as great as 'the sins of the Egyptians, that when God had declared himself by so many signs and wonders on the behalf of the Israelites, that yet notwithstanding, they would still pursue Moses and Israel'.[28] Nor does the forthright way Cromwell dealt with the army disaffection that had surfaced during the last days of the parliamentary session support the view of a man losing control of the reins of power or his old political touch. Before cashiering Packer and the other disaffected officers he confronted a large gathering of army officers with the same political and personal courage he had shown in similar confrontations since the late 1640s. After a dinner at which 'he drank wine very plenteously with them', he delivered a long and, as usual, extempore speech taking his audience through 'the story of our time from 3 Caroli [1628]' onwards, brazenly challenging that anyone who would not conform to his government should come into the open.[29] The episode reveals the elements of cameraderie and iron discipline that had ensured Cromwell's successful control of the army since the Civil War.

Whether Cromwell would have shown the same political strength and determination if he had lived to meet another parliament will, of course, never be known. What suggests that he was not considering the easy route of taking the advice of his civilian, conservative councillors and buying parliamentary political and financial support by granting constitutional concessions is that the 'junta' he appointed in June to prepare for the new parliament had a heavy representation of military advisers who would have opposed strongly that suggestion. It is probable that Cromwell at the end of his life was as unwilling to abandon his vision of taking the country into the promised land as he had ever been, and that he was to the end still determined that, as he said in his last speech to his last parliament, 'liberty of conscience may be secured for honest people, that they may serve God without fear, that every just interest may be preserved, that a godly ministry may be upheld and not to be affronted by seducing and seduced spirits, that all men may be preserved in their just rights, whether civil or spiritual'.[30]

. . .

NOTES AND REFERENCES

1. Abbott, vol. IV, p. 473.
2. Abbott, vol. IV, p. 484.
3. Abbott, vol. IV, p. 445.
4. Abbott, vol. IV, pp. 263, 273–4.

5. Abbott, vol. IV, p. 277.
6. Quoted in C.H. Firth, *The Last Years of the Protectorate 1656–58* (2 vols, 1907), vol. I, p. 21.
7. Abbott, vol. IV, p. 301.
8. Abbott, vol. IV, p. 342.
9. Abbott, vol. IV, p. 417.
10. Quoted in Firth, *Last Years*, vol. I, p. 88.
11. Quoted in Firth, *Last Years*, vol I, p. 89.
12. Abbott, vol. IV, p. 366.
13. Abbott, vol. IV, p. 417.
14. Abbott, vol. IV, pp. 453, 490.
15. *TSP*, vol. IV, p. 93.
16. J.P. Kenyon (ed.), *The Stuart Constitution: Documents and Commentary* (Cambridge University Press, 2nd edn, 1986), p. 329.
17. Abbott, vol. IV, p. 445.
18. Abbott, vol. IV, p. 509.
19. *TSP*, vol. IV, pp. 219, 243.
20. Quoted in Firth, *Last Years*, vol. I, p. 177.
21. Abbott, vol. IV, p. 448.
22. Abbott, vol. IV, p. 443.
23. Abbott, vol. IV, p. 473.
24. Abbott, vol. IV, p. 716.
25. R. Hutton, *The British Republic 1649–60* (Macmillan, 1990), p. 77.
26. D. Underdown, 'Cromwell and the officers, February 1658', *English Historical Review*, **83**, 1968, p. 104.
27. Abbott, vol. IV, p. 729.
28. Quoted in Firth, *Last Years*, vol. II, p. 86.
29. Abbott, vol. IV, p. 736.
30. Abbott, vol. IV, p. 720.

Chapter 8

CONCLUSION

To attempt to assess what Cromwell had achieved by the time he died in 1658 and the ways in which his rule as Protector affected the future course of British history is to enter a minefield of historical controversy and uncertainty. Even during his lifetime, disagreements about his record as ruler were marked. Leveller pamphleteers such as Richard Overton had no doubt that Cromwell was the worst type of Machiavellian hypocrite. 'You shall scarce speak to Crumwell about any thing', wrote Overton in 1649, 'but he will lay his hand on his breast, elevate his eyes and call God to record, he will weep, howl and repent, even while he doth smite you under the first rib.'[1] Some were even more damning, claiming that Cromwell had achieved power 'over head and ears in blood . . . He cares not to spill the blood of his Subjects like water, plenty wherof was shed in our streets, during his short and troublesome Reign, by his oppression, dissimulation, hypocrisies and cruelties'.[2] Other contemporaries, however, had different views. Andrew Marvell, in his *Poem Upon the Death of Oliver Cromwell,* wrote:

Oh! humane glory, vaine, oh! death, oh! wings,
Oh! worthlesse world! oh transitory things!
Yet dwelt that greatnesse in his shape decay'd,
That still though dead, greater than death he lay'd.

In the centuries after his death, opinion about Cromwell has remained deeply divided. In the early years of this century George V refused to allow a new battleship to be named *Cromwell,* while in 1960 Wallingford Borough Council vetoed the name Cromwell Gardens for a road on a new housing estate, on the grounds that 'We have more than

enough benefactors whose names we would like to commemorate without entertaining a malefactor of his class.'[3]
For others, though, Cromwell has been (and still is) a
hero, as he was for a nineteenth-century Newcastle noncon-
formist, Joseph Cowen. Cowen harked back to the seventeenth century in a speech urging an alliance of dissenters
and Liberals to secure religious and civil liberties:

> This country was once ruled by nonconformists and . . .
> never in her history was her influence greater or her
> power more respected (Cheers)...His [Cromwell's] auth-
> ority at home was as potent and effective as it was abroad
> . . . Achievements in the past had won for it the renown
> of history and the gratitude of the nation and there was
> still a nobler future in reserve if its adherents walked in
> the way of their forefathers (Loud cheers)'.[4]

In our own day the group that gathers around Cromwell's
statue outside the Houses of Parliament in London every
year on the anniversary of his death, 3 September, includes
some who commemorate Cromwell as the father of English
parliamentary liberties.

The aim of this final chapter is to emphasise that the
answer to what, on the face of it, is a simple and straightforward question – what were Cromwell's achievements
and legacy? – cannot be either simple or straightforward. It
is undeniable that his achievements fell far short of the
aims he strove for throughout his political career, and that
after his death there was a violent reaction against what he
had done and what he had stood for. Yet, it would be a
mistake to portray his rule as Protector as a total failure
and his effect on subsequent British history as solely negative. Marked though the reaction against Cromwell and
Cromwellian rule was in Restoration England, this should
not be allowed to obliterate Cromwell's achievements as
ruler of Britain and the positive effects his rule had on the
development of the country after his death.

Cromwell's most signal failure was his inability to advance significantly the godly reformation, the pursuit of
which had been the central aim of his career. Like other
godly men and women who since the later sixteenth century had worked for the 'reformation of manners', he also
found that this cause was one supported only by a small

minority. It is not difficult to see why, even in the period before 1640, the campaign to reform, amongst other things, people's morals and to suppress popular festivities and recreations, Sunday sports and alehouses did not gain widespread popular support. What is more, during the 1640s and 1650s the godly cause became even less popular, especially but not only among the propertied, as it became tainted by association with radical social and political ideas, as well as with the political revolution carried out by the army in 1648–49. In 1656 Cromwell claimed that the major-generals' experiment had 'been very effectual towards the discountenancing of vice and settling religion, than anything else these fifty years'.[5] It may be that Cromwell was tacitly admitting that the godly had hitherto achieved little, but his main intention was to claim that the major-generals had been very successful in pursuit of the 'reformation of manners'. This is a judgement that has not been upheld by historical research on the English localities in the 1650s.

It is true that many of the major-generals shared Cromwell's zeal for godly reformation. They had, after all, been appointed by him in consultation with his Council and, as has been seen, an essential part of their instructions, in the wake of the Western Design fiasco, was to bring about moral reform. Charles Worseley, one of the most dynamic major-generals (for Cheshire, Lancashire and Staffordshire) shared Cromwell's desperate desire to root out sins following the disaster in the Caribbean; 'the Lord help us to know what our sin is, or what his pleasure is, that we are so crossed and visited in Jamaica',[6] he wrote. Nor did this kind of zeal meet with a complete lack of response in the localities. The major-generals' correspondence hints at their relief at finding a few 'honest' allies in the localities – 'the good people', 'the best of people', 'the people of God' are some of their descriptions of godly individuals who welcomed the support of the major-generals in their long-running moral campaign.[7] But the stark fact is that the major-generals and their godly allies were in a minority and were pursuing an unpopular cause. The normal local government machinery of justices of the peace, moreover, remained in place, staffed by local men who resented the interference of outsiders in their affairs and who were able to use their local knowledge to frustrate the ambitions of even the most industrious major-general. This did not make the major-generals any the less unpopular, but their reforming impact on England was very slight indeed.

Cromwell also failed to persuade the parliamentary classes that there could be a relaxation of the penal laws enforcing religious uniformity without disturbing the existing social and political order. In fact, if anything, the belief in the necessity of enforcing religious uniformity as a means of maintaining social and political stability increased in strength in the 1650s, as the case of James Nayler demonstrates. The activities of Quakers like Nayler did much to strengthen the opposition of conservative gentry and orthodox church ministers against Cromwell's and the Council's intentions to relax the penal laws and to allow religious groups who did not challenge the authority of the scriptures or commit violent disorders in churches to worship freely. The fact that Cromwellian England did allow a greater degree of religious freedom than ever before, without subverting the existing social order, did not remove the fear of many propertied people that social subversion was only just round the corner. Reports of Quaker violence and Ranter extremism that received much publicity in the 1650s helped Cromwell's opponents to smear Independent religious groups like the Baptists and Presbyterians as potential threats to social and political order. The religious bigotry stimulated among MPs by the Nayler case was a foretaste of the escalating intolerance that exploded after 1660, when attempts to erect a comprehensive English Church were overturned. The Restoration Church Settlement of the early 1660s created a narrow, intolerant Church, from which 'moderate' Protestants, such as Presbyterians and Baptists, as well as 'radical' Protestants such as Quakers, were excluded and, in some cases, savagely persecuted by the legislation known as the Clarendon Code passed by the Cavalier Parliament in the early 1660s.

Equally disappointing, as far as Cromwell was concerned, was the splintering of Protestant unity that occurred in the 1650s and the growth of separate religious sects that were strongly intolerant of the views of each other. As has been seen, Cromwell was not concerned with the development of varying forms of Church government: what concerned him was the disintegration of a universal Protestant brotherhood. Under Cromwell's 'good constable' regime, religious fragmentation is not surprising, but many times he made clear that what was happening ran counter to his aims of maintaining 'a unity of spirit' among Christians and preventing a splintering into a bewildering array of Protestant sects.

Only a little more progress was made towards achieving another of his major aims: the creation of a more socially just society by, above all, reforming the law. Again Cromwell's idealism was thwarted by conservative obstructionism – this time by the vested interests of lawyers and those who feared that tampering with existing legal institutions would be the thin end of the wedge that would open up floodgates of wild and radical schemes devised by the Fifth Monarchy Men and others who agitated for the wholesale destruction of the English institutional and common law structure and its replacement by the Mosaic Law. Just as extremist action by the Quakers made more difficult than ever Cromwell's intention of accomplishing even a moderate extension of religious liberty, so the demands of the Fifth Monarchists allowed the opponents of his policies for moderate reform of the existing legal system to gain sufficient support to frustrate him.

What made Cromwell's reforming aims so difficult to achieve is that they were tainted not just with Quaker and Fifth Monarchy extremism but with hatred of the army. Dislike of the army is a permanent feature of the history of the 1640s and 1650s, rooted in part in the high taxation that was necessary for its upkeep and in the centralised government which had been erected to support the parliamentary war effort. By the 1650s the army was also associated with political radicalism. As has been seen, a (perhaps the) major reason for the trouble Cromwell had with Protectorate parliaments was the fear and hatred some MPs had of the army.[8] Yet Cromwell's failures to achieve his most deeply held aims are not explicable *solely* in terms of the paranoid fears of gentry, lawyers and orthodox ministers. Cromwell himself contributed directly to his own failure. As has been seen, he rarely pursued his aims with consistency. This does not conflict with two central contentions of this book: that Cromwell was, *at times*, much more

164

ruthless and more willing to disregard civil rights and post-pone meetings of 'free' parliaments than has often been realised and that he never abandoned his commitment to his vision of godly reformation. Yet, he was no archetypal military dictator. As has been seen, he punctuated periods of authoritarian rule with attempts at 'healing and settling', when he paid more attention to cultivating conservative support for the regime than to promoting reformation. Cromwell's occasional political excursions into 'healing and settling' (the months after the king's execution in 1649, on his return to London after the battle of Worcester in 1651, and the months after his accession as Protector are some, but not all, of these occasions) must be added to the reasons why he failed to transform England into the New Jerusalem he hoped to achieve.

Yet Cromwell's political skill and adroitness ensured that, although many of his hopes and expectations associated with godly reformation and 'commonwealth' ideals that have been outlined in chapter 5 were largely disappointed, his regime was by no means a total failure. His major political achievement was to make republican government acceptable in a country in which monarchical government was overwhelmingly the one most people preferred. There was no widespread enthusiastic support for the regime, but nor was there much support for royalist opposition to it. The fact that republican government did eventually collapse and that the monarchy was restored in 1660 has tended to cause the history of the 1650s to be portrayed as a country seething with hostility to Cromwell and the republic culminating in the great anti-republican, pro-Royalist explosion in 1660. Though the provincial history of England in the 1650s has not been extensively studied, what seems nearer the truth is that Cromwell ruled a country that gradually became reconciled to the fact that republican government did work at least as effectively as had monarchical government before it. Many of the powerful gentry of England – the people on whose support every early modern regime depended in order to operate successfully – remained fearfully anxious that Cromwell's connections with the army and his repeated statements in favour of religious liberty posed a threat to the social and political order, and to some it seemed as if, in the activities of the Quakers, this threat was becoming a reality. But slowly during the 1650s many of them began to accept, grudgingly in many cases, that republican government suited their requirements: it provided, above all, political stability in England and proved itself capable of efficiently handling the country's affairs in the wider world, in international diplomacy, as well as in Ireland and Scotland.

It would be misleading to exaggerate the extent to which the major gentry families of England accepted Cromwellian rule. By 1653 many of them had voluntarily withdrawn from their traditional role as governors of the English provinces and many that remained were forcibly excluded by the purges of the commissions of the peace carried out by Barebones Parliament. The mood of many gentry remained dominated by fearful forebodings not only of the social consequences of moves towards religious liberty, but also of the revolutionary threat they saw in Cromwell's association with the army, and which was emphasised by the presence in some localities of military garrisons and especially by the appointment as JPs of military men. The compound of anxieties that all this posed a major threat to the traditional social and political structure of the country never disappeared in the 1650s. Cromwell's refusal, even in 1657, to cut his links with the army saw to that. Yet in provincial England during the course of the 1650s Cromwell's moderate 'healing and settling' aims did meet with much more success than did his idealistic pursuit of godly reformation.

What was especially attractive to conservative, propertied people about the government of England under Cromwell is that it filled the main function that was expected of all early modern government: the maintenance of social order and stability. By the early 1650s this task was far from easy. The years immediately following the Civil War had witnessed one of the longest and worst economic crises of the sixteenth and seventeenth centuries, as the harvest failed in successive years between 1646 and 1650. The consequences were disastrous: high food prices, near famine conditions, escalating poverty, food riots and (in the minds of the propertied) incipient popular rebellion. The crisis was made even worse by the demobilisation of soldiers who sought employment and, above all, by the fact that the poor relief system that had developed in the later sixteenth and early seventeenth centuries to cope with this kind of situation had been badly disrupted by the Civil War.

Yet in the 1650s, in every county that has been studied, the local governors responded efficiently to the crisis. In Warwickshire the work undertaken by JPs increased dramatically in the 1650s. Interregnum magistrates carried out three times the amount of work concerning poor relief than had their predecessors in the reign of Charles I; and in Cheshire JPs coped well with the massive increase in the number of poor brought about by the post-war economic crisis and demobilisation of soldiers. They also dealt efficiently with the task of reducing grain prices and ensuring that grain was not hoarded by profiteers. In both these counties, too, magistrates responded to the massive increase in taxation levels that occurred during the Civil War by searching for greater fairness as well as increased yields, basing their demands for money on more accurate valuations of wealth than in the past. No doubt further research on the (as yet) fairly dark world of the English provinces in the 1650s will qualify this picture and reveal elements of continuity in English local government that are much less favourable: corruption, inefficiency and, most likely, a failure to sustain for any length of time governmental activity at the kind of level that was reached in some counties for brief periods in the 1650s. But at the very least the government of the country probably seemed no worse in Cromwellian times than it did at other times in the sixteenth and seventeenth centuries, and at best it may have been better. What is certain is that while Oliver Cromwell lived, local government did not collapse under the weight of opposition to the republic, making the restoration of monarchical government inevitable.

The contribution of Cromwell and the Council to the stability and efficiency of the government of England in the 1650s is, of course, limited. Their personal interventions in favour of 'healing and settling' and reform were spasmodic and did not amount to a co-ordinated 'policy' of centralisation; nor did they have the bureaucratic machinery to carry one out. Indeed some recent work suggests that the main pressure for reform of local government institutions – like the grand juries – came from the localities

167

and not from the Protector or Council. Moreover, since Cromwell was not willing to abandon his aims of a godly reformation, he did not exclude all religious radicals and military men from the bench even when the commissions of the peace were remodelled in 1657. Yet many times in the 1650s he made it clear that he wanted the traditional ruling families to resume an active role in English government, and gradually some of them responded. The most important illustration of this is the way in which during the Protectorate, the commission of the peace in many English counties began once again to include representatives of pre-Civil War ruling elites: a Pelham returning to the Sussex Bench and a Wyndham, a Luttrell and a Rogers becoming JPs again in Somerset. Future research on English localities in the 1650s may modify David Underdown's account but is unlikely to destroy his conclusion that by the last years of the Protectorate 'the country gentry could feel that they were recovering their powers and the local independence that had traditionally been their due'.[9] Moreover, to the intense frustration of Royalist emigrés on the Continent, their appeals for a national uprising against the republic met with hardly any positive response. It is likely that it was not just cowardice or a judicious concern to protect their property and lives that caused wealthy English gentlemen to give no more support to the exiled Charles Stuart in the 1650s than their successors gave later Royalist pretenders, the Jacobite Stuarts in the early eighteenth century. Like the gentlemen of Hanoverian England, the gentry of Cromwellian England realised that the existing regime suited them and their interests too much to risk all on a desperate, reckless gamble in support of a penniless Stuart adventurer.

Cromwell's record in his handling of affairs abroad and in the rest of Britain is in some respects a similar one to his achievement in England: dismal failure judged by his idealistic aims, but considerable achievement judged by the standards of *realpolitik*. Few contemporaries or later commentators (though some have been critical of what Cromwell did) have disputed his success in achieving at least two of the perennial aspirations of English diplomats across the ages: to enhance the country's international reputation and to preserve its security against foreign invasion. One of the most fascinating aspects of this success is that it was achieved by men who were inexperienced in international diplomacy. 'I am apt to think, he [Cromwell] was not guilty of too much knowledge of them [foreign affairs]', wrote a later critic, Slingsby Bethel, with some justice.[10] In 1655 the Brandenburg ambassador, Johann Friedrich Schlezer, felt it necessary to educate Cromwell about Baltic diplomacy by means of a short lecture with maps. Others commented on the lack of experience in international diplomacy among Cromwellian councillors. In August 1655 Cromwell confided to a Swedish ambassador in London, Christer Bonde, that 'it was a matter of grief to him that he had been so ill-educated that he scarcely ventures to speak any other language than English'. A year later Bonde was shocked to learn that, after the departure of Philip Meadowes to Portugal, few in the Cromwellian entourage were proficient in one of the main languages of diplomacy. 'It is a scandal', he wrote, 'they have no one who can write a decent line of Latin, but the blind Miltonius must translate anything they want done from English to Latin, and one can easily imagine how it goes'.[11] Even Bulstrode Whitelocke, who was employed by Cromwell on diplomatic work, including an embassy to Sweden, habitually referred to the Treaty of Osnabruck of 1648 as the Treaty of Augsburg.

Nevertheless Cromwell and his councillors gained a great contemporary international reputation for the republic. Even a hostile observer like the Royalist Sir Edward Hyde, earl of Clarendon, writing after the Restoration, admitted that Cromwell's

> greatness at home was but a shadow of the glory he had abroad. It was hard to discover which feared him most, France, Spain, or the Low Countries, where his friendship was current at the value he put upon it. And as they did all sacrifice their honour and interest at his pleasure, so there is nothing he could have demanded that either of them would have denied him.[12]

When English ambassadors first went abroad, immediately after the establishment of the republic, many of them were shunned by respectable international opinion as representatives of an illegal regicide regime. At least two ambassadors were assassinated in 1649. Yet within a few years, certainly after Cromwell became Protector in 1653, most of the major powers of Europe thought highly enough of the republic to seek to secure it as a friend and ally.

That is, though, the limit of the agreement about the nature of Cromwell's foreign policy. Just after the Restoration, Slingsby Bethel's critique of it for allegedly pursuing Cromwell's religious aims at the expense of England's national interests began a debate that has still not been resolved: was Cromwellian foreign policy dominated by anachronistic religious aims? Did Cromwell pursue aims that were against England's true national interests?

It would be foolish to deny that Cromwell's general hopes in international affairs were centred on religious concerns. The religious zeal with which he argued for the Western Design in 1654 and against the antichristian popery of Spain in the parliamentary session of autumn 1657 has already been noted.[13] He often referred nostalgically to Gustavus Adolphus's campaigns in Europe in the Thirty Years' War as a protestant crusade against Catholic tyranny. Another Swedish ambassador, Peter Julius Coyet, reported to Gustavus's successor, Charles X, that Cromwell 'spoke much' of Gustavus Adolphus, saying

> . . . he had always followed his great campaigns with the greatest pleasure, had many times thanked God, with tears of joy in his eyes [as has been seen Cromwell wept very freely], for His gracious mercies, and when the tidings came of his death, had so mourned it that he could scarcely believe that any Swede could mourn it more bitterly, for he saw that a great instrument to quell the power of the papists had been taken away.

He hoped that Charles X 'would repair that loss . . . he made no doubt that on his side there was a readiness to contribute all possible means to the securing of this work'.[14]

However, two notes of caution need to be sounded before accepting that these aspirations substantiate Bethel-type critiques of Cromwell's foreign policy. Both stem from the fact that 'Cromwell's foreign policy' is a misleading way to describe the handling of foreign affairs during the Protectorate. The first is that (as has been seen) decisions about international affairs were not made solely by Cromwell, but in consultation with his Council. The second is that 'policy' in the sense of a coherent series of decisions based on carefully considered consistent principles does not reflect the way in which diplomacy was conducted during the Protectorate (and maybe at any time). Decisions were made under great pressure when Cromwell and his advisers and councillors were burdened with many other issues, and desperately tired as well as overworked – as foreign ambassadors commented on several occasions. Cromwell, reported Bonde on 18 April 1656, 'had been sitting from morning till night with some of the council, discussing matters of importance, and had not given himself time to eat or drink'.[15] Later, in June 1656, Cromwell and his advisers dealt with foreign affairs in the midst of the great debate with the major-generals about recalling parliament. 'They are so fully occupied', wrote the Venetian ambassador at about this time of Cromwell and his councillors, 'that they do not know which way to turn, and the protector has not a moment to call his own'.[16] Much the same, though, was probably true of any time in the Protectorate.

In these circumstances a more useful approach to the handling of foreign affairs in this period is the one suggested by J.H. Elliott, when writing about the government of France and Spain:

> The traditional formulation of the foreign policy motivation of early seventeenth-century statesmen in terms of confessionalism or *raison d'état* may . . . be misconceived. [Richelieu and Olivares] could adhere to neither of these extreme positions. They were forced to operate as best they could in a grey area of compromise, casuistry and equivocation, weighing political advantage against religious scruple and the dictates of conscience.[17]

The political skills Cromwell had acquired since his days as a naive MP in 1640–41 made him well-suited to the world of international diplomacy described in that quotation. Decisions were made by Cromwell and others, often in haste, and always for a mixture of complex motives; and never only because of either religious ideology or national interest.

Cromwellian relations with the Dutch were certainly governed by a mixture of motives. Slingsby Bethel considered that the Treaty of Westminster, which ended the Anglo-Dutch war in April 1654, was 'damageable' to English interests because Cromwell was led by his hopes of creating an alliance of protestant nations to make peace with England's major trading rival on too lenient terms. Yet Cromwell and the Council were driven by other considerations as well as by religion in the negotiations with the Dutch. They were especially concerned not to revive Orange–Stuart friendships and so prompt the Dutch into helping a Royalist invasion of England. The Dutch even agreed to a secret clause being inserted in the treaty committing them never to allow a member of the Orange family to become a Stadholder of the United Provinces. Cromwell and his advisers were also aware that, if the war had continued, the Dutch might ally with Denmark and thereby secure trading privileges in the Baltic to the detriment of English merchants there. Peace with the Dutch in fact reopened the Baltic to English shipping and soon afterwards Cromwellian ambassadors secured an Anglo-Danish commercial treaty that gave English ships equal rights with the Dutch when passing into the Baltic through the Sound.

Nor should English relations with Spain in the 1650s be seen in terms of ideology *versus* national interest. Alongside the undoubted religious zeal that persuaded him to argue in Council for war against Spain were Cromwell's hopes of profiting from the capture of Spanish treasure ships and of making the navy, unemployed after the Dutch war, pay for itself by giving empoyment to the redundant '160 sail of brave ships well appointed swimming at sea'. Security, too, was as usual uppermost in the minds of the Protector and his advisers, and it maybe that what swung opinion in the Council, after much debate, towards a *rapprochement* (first by a defensive treaty made in October 1655) with France and war with Spain was that France was a much more dangerous launching pad for a Stuart invasion of England than the more distant shores of Spain. When relations with France were further cemented by an offensive treaty in March 1657, high on the Cromwellian agenda was the hope that a joint campaign against the Spanish in Flanders would lead to the capture of Dunkirk (which came about in June 1658) and so provide a useful counter to any

Stuart-Spanish threats to English security from across the Channel.

Cromwell's dreams of one day supporting Charles X as a latter-day Gustavus Adolphus on a protestant crusade against the Catholics of southern Europe and his close friendship with the Swedish ambassadors in London, Bonde and Coyet, have led some to depict Cromwell as being duped by wily diplomats who played on his religious aspirations. In fact a reading of the correspondence of the Swedish ambassadors with Charles X makes clear that Cromwell and his councillors were adept at resisting tempting Swedish offers to enter an alliance with Sweden, thus allowing Charles X to dominate the Baltic. An Anglo-Swedish trade treaty was signed in July 1656, but the negotiations for a fuller alliance were never concluded. Cromwell and his advisers refused to take sides in the developing quarrel between Sweden and Denmark that flared into open war in 1657; and Cromwell, through his ambassador, Philip Meadowes, played a key role in bringing about peace in the Baltic by the Treaty of Roskilde in February 1658, which preserved a balance between Sweden, Denmark, England and the Dutch in that trading area so vital to all these northern nations.

What is clearer and less controversial than the motives behind English foreign policy in the 1650s is the forthright way in which Cromwell and his councillors used armed force as well as diplomatic influence in international affairs. Bernard Capp's recent study of the Cromwellian navy makes clear that Cromwell continued a policy begun by the Rump of building an extraordinarily powerful naval force. In 1655 Protector and councillors were present at the launching of a new ship *The Naseby*, which the Royalist Sir John Evelyn noted had as its figurehead 'Oliver on horseback, trampling six nations under foot, a Scot, Irishman, Dutch, French, Spaniard and English . . . a Fame held a laurel over his insulting head, and the Word, "God with Us"'.[18] The history of the Cromwellian navy under the leadership of Robert Blake is punctuated with dazzling victories – such as the bold attack on Port Farina attempting to rescue English prisoners captured by the Bey of Tunis and North African pirates in April 1655 and the destruction of the returning Spanish treasure fleet at Santa Cruz in the Canary Islands two years later. English foreign affairs under Cromwell were far from being totally successful, but they were conducted with a vigour that preserved the security and enhanced the international reputation of the English Republic.

Or should it be 'the British Republic'? Certainly during the Protectorate Ireland and Scotland were brought into a closer union with England and Wales than ever before. Yet what was achieved in the 1650s fell far short of the Cromwellian ideal of a British Republic united as a godly society. English relations with Ireland and Scotland reflect (as do other aspects of Cromwell's rule) a mixture of Cromwellian ideals combined with realistic pragmatism.

As has been seen, there were great differences in his attitudes to both countries. Like the Rump, which in 1652 had passed an act decreeing the death penalty for all in Ireland who had supported 'the rebellion' against England (estimated by S.R. Gardiner at about 100,000 out of an adult male, Catholic Irish population of 180,000),[19] he considered Ireland to be a conquered country on which English rule should be ruthlessly imposed. Also like others in the Commonwealth and Protectorate governments, he believed that this should be accompanied by the confiscation from Irish landowners of millions of acres of land, which were either to be granted to those like himself, who, since 1641 had lent money to subsidise the Irish 'adventure', or to compensate English soldiers for wage arrears. The dispossessed Irish landowners, together with their tenants, servants and labourers, were to be transplanted forcibly to designated areas of western Ireland, largely in Connaught and Clare, leaving the land free for mass settlement by the English and the Scots. Scotland, on the other hand, Cromwell considered was not a conquered country but one the English had reluctantly invaded in order to bring about a 'union and right understanding between the godly people', the English and 'our brethren of Scotland'.[20] Yet, despite the differences for both countries, Cromwell's main hope for them was the same: that they should become the kind of godly societies that he wanted to develop in England. In 1649, as has been seen, he wrote that conquered Ireland should be a testing ground for the New Jerusalem that was to be built in England. The ordinances he and his Council issued in April 1654, uniting England and Scotland, were a step on the way to persuade the Scots to overthrow those who stood in the way of bringing about in their country a Cromwellian and English godly reformation. The preamble to one of the ordinances made clear that the intention behind the union was that 'the people of Scotland be made equal sharers with those of England in the present Settlement of Peace, Liberty and Property' and 'the Mercies which it hath pleased God to give to this Nation [England]'.[21]

What happened in Ireland and Scotland in the 1650s was far removed from these aspirations. Indeed, developments in 'Cromwellian Scotland' and 'Cromwellian Ireland' had very little to do with Oliver Cromwell, who, pressed as he was by problems elsewhere, left the rule of both countries to others. Cromwell's elder son, Henry, was from the end of December 1654 the main influence in Irish affairs, and it was General Monk, as commander-in-chief of the army in Scotland, and Lord Broghill, as president of the Council of Scotland in 1656, who shaped English policies north of the border. These men ensured that Cromwellian ideals were greatly moderated by the pressing considerations they faced in both countries. By Cromwell's death, despite the high price, both in terms of money and in Irish and Scottish resentment, the best that can be said is that a united British Republic had become a temporary reality.

Cromwell headed a republican government that, in the face of constant distrust on the part of the gentry and mounting financial debt, ran the country at least as well as monarchical regimes before and since. The same cannot be said of those who succeeded him. The story of the twenty months after Cromwell's death is one of the utter failure of his successors to do what he had done. Neither Richard Cromwell nor the army generals who came after him were able to prevent the collapse of republican government in England by the winter of 1659–60. But it is important to stress that this happened after Oliver Cromwell's death and not before.

The anarchic situation that had developed within a year of his death produced the support for the restoration of the monarchy which had not been in existence while

Oliver Cromwell lived. Yet Cromwell had never gained widespread support and the Restoration triggered a violent reaction against him and what he had stood for. Within days of Charles II's entry into London from his long exile, effigies of Cromwell were burnt on bonfires in London, and a Cromwellian puppet hung by the neck from a window in the royal palace in Whitehall became the focus of 'the populace who thronged to see it and [they] spared no act of contempt or ignominy'.[22] On 30 January 1661, in a gruesome ceremony to mark the anniversary of Charles I's death, Cromwell's body and those of his mother and associates such as Broghill and Ireton were exhumed and hung on the gallows at Tyburn. All this was accompanied in the early 1660s by a violent campaign against Dissenters and the erection by parliament of a system of religious apartheid which attempted to exclude Dissenters from every avenue of public life.

Was, then, the only legacy of Cromwellian rule a negative reaction against standing armies, against Dissenters, against republican government, all of which are strong themes of the history of post-Cromwellian England? Cromwell's political career did have one positive lasting effect on the future development of the country. It was, ironically, one that Cromwell would undoubtedly have not wanted: the establishment of Protestant nonconformity as a permanent feature of life in Britain from that day to this. As has been seen, Cromwell had tried to prevent the growth of nonconformity by keeping most religious groups within a national Church. Nor was he without support. People like Richard Baxter, who had originally opposed Cromwell, came to support his pan-protestant aims. Baxter's Worcestershire Association was a model for other co-operative associations of ministers and congregations of different types: 'men of no faction nor siding with any party, but owning that which was good in all as far as they could discuss it'.

At the Restoration these hopes of a comprehensive national Protestant Church in England were blasted. But the dominant militant intolerance exhibited in the early 1660s did not obliterate the Protestant diversity that had blossomed in Cromwellian England. Despite the Clarendon Code the heirs of late sixteenth- and early seventeenth-century godly Puritans, Presbyterians, Independents, Congregationalists, Baptists and Quakers survived 'the experience of defeat' in Restoration England. Like their godly forbears of the period before 1640 they remained a minority in English society. Even in the early eighteenth century, a survey by nonconformists concluded that they amounted to only about 6 per cent of the population of England and Wales. Yet they survived (known as 'Dissenters' and later as 'Nonconformists') to play a major role, first in British commercial life and later in most major areas of British politics and society as well. It is perhaps fitting that the man who was catapulted into becoming a political activist by his religious views, and who was driven by religious zeal to rise from his origins as an East Anglian farmer to be ruler of Britain, should have left as his major legacy an indelible religious imprint on the development of his country.

.   .   .

NOTES AND REFERENCES

1. D.M.Wolfe (ed.), *Leveller Manifestoes of the Puritan Revolution* (Thomas Nelson and Sons, 1944), p. 370.
2. Quoted in R. Howell, 'Cromwell and English liberty' in R.C. Richardson and G.M. Ridden (eds), *Freedom and the English Revolution* (Manchester University Press, 1986), p. 25.
3. Ibid., p 26.
4. Quoted in R. Howell, *Puritans and Radicals in North England: Essays in the English Revolution* (University Press of America, 1984), pp. 207–8.
5. Abbott, vol. IV, p. 274.
6. Quoted in A. Fletcher, 'The religious motivation of Cromwell's major-generals' in D. Baker (ed.), *Religious Motivation: Biographical and Sociological Problems for the Church Historian* (Studies in Church History, vol. XV, 1978), p. 261.
7. Quoted in A. Fletcher, 'Oliver Cromwell and the localities: the problem of consent' in C. Jones, M. Newitt and S. Roberts, (eds), *Politics and People in Revolutionary England* (Blackwell, 1986), p. 92.
8. This is one of many important points made in a good unpublished study by S. Jones, 'The Composition and Activity of the Protectorate Parliaments' (Exeter University Ph.D thesis, 1988). I am very grateful to Dr Jones

for kindly lending me a copy of her thesis.

9. D. Underdown, 'Settlement in the counties' in G.E. Aylmer, (ed.), *The Interregnum: The Quest for Settlement 1646–60* (Macmillan, 1972), p. 178.

10. Slingsby Bethel, *The World's Mistake in Oliver Cromwell*, printed in W. Oldys (ed.), *Harleian Miscellany; or a Collection of Scarce, Curious and Entertaining Tracts . . .* (10 vols, 1808–13), vol. I, p. 289.

11. M. Roberts (ed.), *Swedish Diplomats at Cromwell's Court 1655–56: the Missions of Peter Julius Coyet and Christer Bonde* (Camden Society, 4th series, vol. 36, 1988), pp. 114, 282.

12. Clarendon, *History,* vol. VI, p. 94.

13. See pp. 133, 143.

14. Roberts, *Swedish Diplomats,* pp. 83–4.

15. Ibid., p. 278.

16. Quoted in ibid., p. 278, note.

17. J.H. Elliott, *Richelieu and Olivares* (Oxford University Press, 1984), p. 128.

18. Quoted in B. Capp, *Cromwell's Navy: the Fleet and the English Revolution* (Clarendon Press, 1989), p. 5.

19. Gardiner, *Commonwealth,* vol. IV, p. 83, note.

20. Abbott, vol. I, pp. 177–8.

21. Firth and Rait, *Acts and Ordinances,* vol. II, p. 875.

22. Quoted in T. Harris, *London Crowds in the Reign of Charles II: Propaganda and Politics from the Restoration to the Exclusion Crisis* (Cambridge University Press, 1987), p. 39.

LIST OF DATES

25 April 1599	Oliver Cromwell born in Huntingdon.
1616–1617	Studied at University of Cambridge.
1617	Death of Cromwell's father.
1620	Married Elizabeth Bourchier.
1628	Elected MP for Huntingdon.
1630	Took part in quarrel over Huntingdon town charter.
1631	Sold property in Huntingdon and moved to St Ives.
1636	Moved to Ely, where he had inherited his uncle's house and property.
1640	Elected MP for Cambridge in both of this year's parliamentary elections.
1640–42	Backbench MP in early sessions of the Long Parliament.
1 Nov. 1641	News of Irish Rebellion reached London.
4 Jan. 1642	Charles I's attempted arrest of the Five Members and Lord Kimbolton.
Aug. 1642	Raised troop of soldiers with his brother-in-law, Valentine Walton, and ambushed a Royalist convoy outside Cambridge.
22 Aug. 1642	Official start of the Civil War.
22 Oct. 1642	Served with earl of Essex at the battle of Edgehill.

Jan. 1643	Appointed captain and sent to join the army of the Eastern Association under Lord Grey of Warke for the defence of East Anglia.
Spring–summer 1643	Took part in minor skirmishes in Eastern England against Royalist garrisons and outriders of the earl of Newcastle's advancing army. Failed to co-ordinate activities with other parliamentary commanders.
Jan.–Feb. 1644	Supported alliance of Independent peers and middle-group MPs in successfully pushing through parliament a military and financial reorganisation of the army of the Eastern Association under the earl of Manchester. Promoted Lieutenant-General of this army under Manchester.
March 1644	Quarrelled with Lawrence Crawford, a Presbyterian Scot in the Eastern Association army, who had disciplined two men for their religious beliefs.
June 1644	Siege of York.
2 July 1644	Defeat of Royalist armies at battle of Marston Moor.
Sept. 1644	Appeared with Crawford before Committee of Both Kingdoms in an effort to settle their quarrel. Supported accommodation order in Commons to allow liberty to tender consciences in a national Church.
Oct.–Nov. 1644	With other generals, blamed Manchester for disastrous military campaign in Berkshire.
Nov.–Dec. 1644	Exchanged charges and countercharges with Manchester in parliament.
9 Dec. 1644	Self-denying ordinance proposed.

Dec. 1644–March 1645	Supported passage of Self-denying ordinance and creation of New Model Army.
March 1645–May 1646	Given exemptions from Self-denying ordinance and resumed military service, mainly under Fairfax. Victories at Naseby (10 June 1645), Langport (July 1645), Bristol (September 1645).
May 1646	End of Civil War.
June 1646	Returned to Westminster.
Oct. 1646	Granted £2,500 p.a. from confiscated estates of marquis of Winchester. Mrs Cromwell and children joined him in London from Ely.
Jan. 1647	Scots handed over Charles I to the English parliament, who lodged him in Holmby House (Northants) in the following month.
Feb.–March 1647	Holles and Political Presbyterians proposed to disband the New Model Army without satisfying its demands.
2–19 May 1647	With Skippon, Ireton and Fleetwood went to Saffron Walden to try to pacify the army.
27 May 1647	With Ireton received wage arrears from parliament.
3 June 1647	Left London to re-join the New Model Army at Newmarket.
4 June 1647	Army's *Solemn Engagement* issued.
16 June 1647	Army's *Remonstrance,* impeaching the Eleven MPs, issued.
July 1647	*The Heads of the Proposals* drafted and then debated by the army Council at Reading.
6 August 1647	After an attempted counter-revolution in London (26 July) the army occupied London.
Aug.–Oct. 1647	With his parliamentary allies negotiated with king on *The Heads of the Proposals.*

18 Oct. 1647	*The Case of the Army* presented to Fairfax.
26 October 1647	The first *Agreement of the People* published.
28 Oct.–8 Nov.1647	The Putney Debates.
11 Nov. 1647	Charles escaped from Hampton Court and fled to the Isle of Wight.
15 Nov. 1647	Suppressed army mutiny at Corkbush Field, Ware, Herts.
Dec. 1647	Charles I made the Engagement with the Scots and rejected parliamentary proposals for a settlement, the Four Bills.
3 Jan. 1648	Supported Commons' Vote of No Addresses.
29 April 1648	Attended the army Council prayer meeting at Windsor.
May–Oct. 1648	Cromwell's army put down a rebellion in South Wales, defeated (with Lambert) an invading Scottish army in Lancashire, and cowed opposition to the English army in Scotland.
Nov. 1648	Remained in the North at the siege of Pontefract, while the army issued a Remonstrance calling for a purge of parliament and the king's trial.
Dec. 1648–Jan. 1649	Arrived in London after Pride's Purge, eventually committing himself to the king's trial and execution and establishment of a republic.
May 1649	With Fairfax put down an army mutiny at Burford (Oxfordshire)
Aug. 1649–May 1650	Led an expeditionary force to Ireland. Major military engagements at Drogheda (Sept. 1649), Wexford (Oct. 1649) and Clonmel (April 1650)
June 1650	Hailed as hero on his return to London, and appointed commander of expeditionary force against

	Scotland after Fairfax turned down the post.
July 1650–Aug. 1651	Second military campaign (with Lambert) in Scotland, including battle of Dunbar (Sept. 1650).
3 Sept. 1651	Battle of Worcester.
20 April 1653	Dissolved the Rump Parliament.
May–June 1653	With army officers appointed members of Barebones Parliament.
4 July 1653	Opened Barebones Parliament.
12 Dec. 1653	Accepted resignation of majority of Barebones Parliament and allowed ejection of the minority who continued to meet.
16 Dec. 1653	Accepted the Instrument of Government and installed as Lord Protector.
19 Jan. 1654	Abandoned the Oath of Engagement.
20 March 1654	With his Council issued the Triers ordinance.
April 1654	Moved with his family into the Palace of Whitehall. Ended the Anglo-Dutch war. With his Council issued the Union with Scotland ordinance.
April, July 1654	Foreign policy debates in the Protectorate Council.
Aug. 1654	With his Council issued the Ejectors and Chancery Reform ordinances.
4 Sept. 1654	Opened first Protectorate parliament.
12 Sept. 1654	With his council forced MPs to sign a 'Recognition'.
Oct. 1654	The Three Colonels' petition presented to him.
Dec. 1654	The Western Design expeditionary force set off to the Caribbean.
March 1655	Penruddock's Rising.
April 1655	Dismissed two judges for questioning a Treason ordinance.

May 1655	News of the Vaudois massacre reached England. Cony's Case heard before the Upper Bench.
June 1655	Resignation of Bulstrode White-locke and Thomas Widdrington, commissioners of the great seal, and Chief Justice Rolle.
24 July 1655	News of the defeat of the Western Design expedition at San Domingo on 25 April reached London.
Aug. 1655	Appointment of the major-generals.
October 1655	Revised ('moral order') instructions given to the major-generals. Anglo-French treaty made and war with Spain begun.
Dec. 1655	The readmission of the Jews to England discussed.
July 1656	Writs issued for the second Protectorate parliament.
Sept. 1656	Naval victory off Cadiz. Opening of second Protectorate parliament after exclusion of a hundred elected MPs.
Dec. 1656	Nayler's case.
Jan.– Feb. 1657	Decided to abandon the Instrument of Government and the major-generals.
March 1657	The Humble Petition and Advice presented to him.
May 1657	Accepted the Humble Petition and Advice but refused the crown. Blake's victory off Santa Cruz in the Canaries.
26 June 1657	His second installation as Lord Protector.
July 1657	Lambert's resignation as major-general.
Dec. 1657	Richard Cromwell brought to London and admitted to the Council.
20 January 1658	Second session of the second Protectorate parliament began.

4 Feb. 1658	Dissolved second Protectorate parliament.
11 Feb. 1658	Cashiered Major Packer and five other officers.
May–June 1658	Trial of Sir Henry Slingsby and Dr John Hewett.
6 Aug. 1658	Death of his daughter, Elizabeth Claypole.
3 Sept. 1658	Death of Oliver Cromwell.

BIBLIOGRAPHICAL ESSAY

Unless stated otherwise the place of publication is London. University Presses are indicated solely by place.

'The general rule', wrote the cynical Thomas Carlyle, in the middle of the nineteenth century, about biographies of Oliver Cromwell, is that 'you can find as many inaccuracies as you like; dig where you please, water will come!' That rule, however, does not apply to most of the many biographies of Cromwell written since Carlyle's day. Given the mountainous obstacles in the way of presenting a balanced picture of him – wildly contrasting views that have been and still are held of him, ambiguous source material and Cromwell's apparently inconsistent character – it is not surprising that none of them can be described as 'definitive'. The biographies that seem to me to get closest to reflecting the 'true' Oliver Cromwell are by S.R. Gardiner, *Oliver Cromwell* (Longmans, Green 1909); C.H. Firth, *Oliver Cromwell and the Rule of the Puritans* (Oxford 1900); R.S. Paul, *The Lord Protector* (Lutterworth Press 1958); and C. Hill, *God's Englishman* (Harmondsworth, Penguin 1970) and 'Oliver Cromwell' in *The Collected Essays of Christopher Hill* (Brighton, Harvester, 3 vols, 1985–86), vol. 3. None of the others are without value, however, and older books like J. Buchan, *Oliver Cromwell* (Hodder and Stoughton 1934) and more recent ones such as P. Gregg, *Oliver Cromwell* (Weidenfeld and Nicolson, 1988) have much to contribute to Cromwellian studies. Judging by its sales and the number of times it is mentioned in conversations with people outside the academic world, A. Fraser, *Cromwell, Our Chief of Men* (Weidenfeld and Nicolson 1973) is the most popular biography. It has the merit of bringing together much material on Cromwell and is more important as a work of reference than of interpretation. Much more obviously a reference book is P. Gaunt, *The Cromwellian Gazeteer* (Gloucester, Alan Sutton,1987), which is a county-by-county guide to sites associated with Cromwell, and it includes a useful itinerary (with maps) of Cromwell's known movements throughout his life.

Among the collections of essays on Cromwell the one edited by J. Morrill, *Oliver Cromwell and the English Revolution* (Longman, 1990) is outstanding; articles from that book are scattered throughout this essay. Two other useful collections of articles are S.R. Gardiner, *Cromwell's Place in History* (Longmans, Green, 1898) and I. Roots, (ed), *Cromwell: a Profile* (Macmillan 1973) . The use of the article format to illuminate Cromwell's character and aims is demonstrated most brilliantly in four essays by B. Worden, 'Toleration and the Cromwellian Protectorate' in W.J. Sheils (ed.), *Persecution and Toleration: Studies in Church History* (Oxford, Blackwell 1984); 'The politics of Marvell's Horation Ode', *Historical Journal*, **7**, 1984; 'Providence and politics in Cromwellian England', *Past and Present*, **109**, 1985; and 'Oliver Cromwell and the sin of Achan' in D. Beales and G. Best (eds), *History, Society and the Churches* (Cambridge, 1985). These are essential reading for anyone interested in the Protector.

The best general book that covers nearly the whole of the period of Cromwell's lifetime is D. Hirst, *Authority and Conflict: England 1603–58* (Arnold, 1985). I. Roots, *The Great Rebellion 1640–60* (Batsford, 1966) and G.E.Aylmer, *Rebellion or Revolution?* (Oxford, 1987) provide clear, readable introductions to the 1640s and 1650s, together with three good collections of essays in the Macmillan Problems in Focus series: C. Russell, (ed.), *The Origins of the English Civil War* (Macmillan, 1973); J. Morrill (ed.), *Reactions to the English Civil War* (Macmillan, 1982) and G.E. Aylmer, (ed.), *The Interregnum: the Quest for Settlement* (Macmillan, 1973). J. Morrill, *The Revolt of the Provinces* (Longman, 2nd edn. 1980) and D. Underdown, *Pride's Purge: Politics in the Puritan Revolution* (Oxford, 1971) present stimulating views of the 1640s. There are three excellent introductions to the history of the 1650s: T. Barnard, *The English Republic* (Longman, 1982): A. Woolrych, *England Without a King* (Lancaster, Methuen, 1983) and R. Hutton, *The British Republic 1649–60* (Macmillan, 1990). For those with more time, though, the best way to approach the history of England during Cromwell's lifetime is by ploughing through S.R. Gardiner's multi-volume *History of England from the Accession of King James I to the Outbreak of the Civil War* (Longmans, Green, 10 Vols, 1882); *History of the Great Civil War* (Longmans, Green, 4 vols, 1893); *History of the Commonwealth and Protectorate* (Longmans, Green, 4 vols, 1903); and C. Firth, *The Last Years of the Protectorate* (Longmans, Green, 2 vols, 1909), which was completed after Gardiner's death.

Until recently little of worth had been written on Cromwell's life before 1640, simply because it was thought that sufficient source material did not exist. This is not something, however, which has prevented J. Morrill, 'The making of Oliver Cromwell' in Morrill, (ed.), *Cromwell* (above) from presenting stimulating new interpretations of the 'prehistoric' Cromwell. His article, and B. Quintrell's, 'Oliver Cromwell and the distraint of knighthood', *Bulletin of the Institute of Historical Research*, **57**, 1984 are by far and away the best studies on Cromwell's career before the calling of the Long Parliament. There is much more to be read on the historical context in which Cromwell spent the first two-thirds of his life. During the last fifteen years or so the history of later sixteenth and early seventeenth century England has been subjected to a great wave of 'revisionism' which has challenged many older assumptions about that period. Good guides to 'revisionist' works, and to those which challenge them, are R. Cust and A. Hughes, 'After revisionism' in R. Cust and A. Hughes (eds), *Conflict in Early Stuart England: Studies in Religion and Politics, 1603–42* (Longman, 1989), R.C. Richardson, *The Debate on the English Revolution Revisited* (Routledge and Kegan Paul, 1988), G. Burgess, 'On Revisionism: an analysis of early Stuart historiography in the 1970s and 1980s', *Historical Journal*, **33**, 1990, and B. Coward, 'Was there an English Revolution in the middle of the seventeenth century?' in C. Jones, M. Newitt and S. Roberts (eds), *Politics and People in Revolutionary England* (Oxford, Blackwell, 1986).

The best recent study of Cromwell's political career in the 1640s is J. Adamson, 'Oliver Cromwell and the Long Parliament', in Morrill (ed.), *Cromwell* (see above). Adamson's concentration on the role of peerage in politics in that article and in 'The *Vindiciae Veritatis* and the political creed of Viscount Saye and Sele' *Historical Journal*, **60**, 1987 (see also his 'The baronial context of the English Civil War', *Transactions of the Royal Historical Society*, 5th series, **40**, 1990; and his forthcoming book, *The Nobility and the English Revolution*, (Oxford)) is important but should not cause older works on the parliamentary politics of the 1640s to be ignored. Underdown, *Pride's Purge* (see above), is especially useful on Cromwell's role in the parliamentary politics of the Civil War. M. Kishlansky, *The Rise of the New Model Army* (Cambridge, 1979), A.N.B. Cotton, 'Cromwell and the self-denying ordinance', *History*, **42**, 1977 and C. Holmes, 'Colonel King and Lincolnshire politics, 1642–46', *Historical Journal*, **16**, 1973 and the documents printed in Bruce, (ed.), *The Quarrel between the earl of Manchester and Oliver Cromwell* (Camden Society, 1875) are also vital for this period. But, if one were to have to select only one book on Cromwell in the mid-1640s, this would be C. Holmes, *The Eastern Association in the English Civil War* (Cambridge, 1975), which presents a persuasive interpretation of Cromwell's career in local and parliamentary politics during the Civil War.

Holmes also bridges the gap that has been created by historians between political and military history and has much of interest on Cromwell's military, as well as political, career. For Cromwell as a soldier, A. Woolrych's article with that title in Morrill (ed.), *Cromwell* (above) is a useful survey. Of modern works, J. Gillingham, *Portrait of a Soldier: Cromwell* (Weidenfeld & Nicolson, 1976) is often unfairly neglected. The following go far towards satisfying those with a yearning to get to grips with military tactics and weaponry in Cromwell's army: A. Woolrych, *Battles of the English Civil War* (Batsford, 1961), and P. Newman, *The Battle of Marston Moor 1644* (A. Bird, Chichester 1981). The 'classic' book on this subject is C.H. Firth, *Cromwell's Army* (1902).

The indispensable book on Cromwell's role in post-Civil War politics is A. Woolrych, *Soldiers and Statesmen: the General Council of the Army and its Debates 1647–48* (Oxford, 1987). J. Morrill, 'The army revolt of 1647' in A.C. Duke and C.A. Tamse (eds), *Britain and the Netherlands* (The Hague, Martinus Nijhoff 1977) and J. Adamson, 'The English nobility and the projected settlement of 1647', *Histori-cal Journal*, **30**, 1987 are also useful on Cromwell's part in the fast-moving events of 1647. The articles by G.E. Aylmer, 'Was Cromwell a member of the army in 1646–7 or not?', *History*, **56**, 1971 and C. Hoover, 'Cromwell's status and pay in 1646-7', *Historical Journal*, **23**, 1980 deal with particularly knotty problems of Cromwell's career at this stage. The best and most accessible collection of primary source ma-terial on Cromwell the politician in this period is A.S.P. Woodhouse (ed.), *Puritanism and Liberty* (Dent, 1983). Vital too is C.H. Firth, (ed.), *The Clarke Papers: Selection from the Papers of William Clarke. . . . 1647–49 . . . and 1651–60* (Royal Historical Society, Camden Society, 2 vols, 1891 and 1893). D. Underdown, 'The parliamentary diary of John Boys 1647–48', *Bulletin of the Institute of Historical Research*, **39**, 1966 prints revealing reports of some of Cromwell's speeches made at a time when evidence of Cromwell's acti-vities is particularly sparse.

The definitive book on the political history of England after the establishment of the Republic is B. Worden, *The Rump Parliament 1648–53* (Cambridge, 1974) which in-cludes many telling insights into Cromwell's aims and acti-vities between the Revolution and the establishment of the Protectorate, as well as into the reasons why Cromwell dis-solved the Rump. A much older work, though its conclu-sions are questioned by Worden, is still useful on this, C.H. Firth, 'Cromwell and the expulsion of the Long Parliament in 1653', *English Historical Review*, **8**, 1893. A. Woolrych, *Commonwealth to Protectorate* (Oxford, 1982, paperback edn, 1986) is a dense book on the tangled politics of 1653, fo-cusing on Barebones Parliament, but it repays careful read-ing since Cromwell's activities are given close scrutiny.

There are no solid studies of politics during the Protec-torate of the stature of Worden's and Woolrych's books on the early years of the Republic. However, of the general books Hirst and Roots (see above) are particularly good on this period and D. Hirst, 'The Lord Protector 1653–58' in Morrill, *Cromwell* (see above) and A. Woolrych, 'The Crom-wellian protectorate: a military dictatorship?', *History*, **75**, 1990 also suggest useful approaches to Cromwell's career as Protector. There is no full published account of par-liamentary politics during the Protectorate (but see S.

Jones, 'The composition and activity of the Protectorate Parliaments', unpublished Exeter Ph.D thesis, 1988). H. R. Trevor-Roper, 'Oliver Cromwell and his parliaments' in Roots (ed.), *Cromwell* (above) is typically provocative and lively; while P. Gaunt takes a more staid and detailed look at 'Law-making in the first protectorate parliament' in C. Jones, M. Newitt and S. Roberts (eds.), *Politics and People* (see above). The politics of the Protectorate parliaments can be followed in Thomas Burton, *Diary* . . . (ed. J. Rutt, 4 vols., 1828; reprint ed. New York, ed. I. Roots, 1974). P.Gaunt's articles emphasise the important role of the Council during the Protectorate: 'Cromwell's purge?: Exclusion in the first protectorate parliament', *Parliamentary History,* **6** 1987 and '"The single person's confidants and dependants": Oliver Cromwell and the protectorate councillors', *Historical Journal,* **36**, 1989, following the line pioneered by his teacher I. Roots, in 'Cromwell's ordinances: the early legislation of the Protectorate' in Aylmer (ed.), *Interregnum* (see above).

The machinery and personnel of central government in the 1650s is studied at length in R. Sherwood, *The Court of Oliver Cromwell* (Croom Helm, 1977) and G.E. Aylmer, *The State's Servants* (Routledge & Kegan Paul, 1973). There are also useful biographies of some of the men around Cromwell: R. Spalding, *The Improbable Puritan: Bulstrode Whitelocke* (Faber and Faber, 1975); N. Matthews, *William Sheppard; Cromwell's Law Reformer* (Cambridge, 1984); R.W. Ramsey, *Henry Cromwell* (Longmans, Green, 1933); V. Rowe, *Sir Henry Vane the Younger* (Athlone Press, 1970); P. Gregg, *Freeborn John: a biography of John Lilburne* (Dent: paperback edn. 1986); J.Scott, *Algernon Sydney and the English Revolution, 1623–77* (Cambridge, 1988); and P. Aubrey, *Mr Secretary Thurloe: Cromwell's Secretary of State 1652–60* (Athlone Press, 1990). Although many historians have made good use of Thurloe's papers, Thomas Birch, (ed.), *A Collection of the State Papers of John Thurloe* (7 vols, 1742) – for example, D. Underdown in *Royalist Conspiracy in England 1649–60* (Archon Books, New Haven, 1960) – they have not yet been fully explored.

Cromwell's interest in law reform is dealt with in D. Veall, *The Popular Movement for Law Reform 1640–60* (Oxford, 1970); and M. Cotterall, 'Interregnum law reform:

the Hale commission of 1652', *English Historical Review*, **83**, 1968.

The most interesting recent work on Cromwell as Protector has concentrated on his religious ideals. For the general context in which to study these see Morrill, 'The Church of England 1642–49' in his *Reactions* (above); C. Cross, 'The Church in England' in Aylmer (ed.), *Interregnum* (above); and W.A. Shaw, *A History of the English Church During the Civil Wars and under the Commonwealth* (2 vols, Longmans, Green, 1900). But the most important works that bear directly on Cromwell's religious beliefs are the articles by Worden (above). R. Howell, 'Cromwell and English liberty' in R.C. Richardson and G.M. Ridden (eds), *Freedom and the English Revolution* (Manchester, 1986), J.C. Davies, 'Cromwell's religion' and A. Fletcher, 'Oliver Cromwell and the godly nation' in Morrill, *Cromwell* (see above) also help to bring these beliefs into sharper focus. D.S. Katz, *Philo-semitism and the Readmission of the Jews to England 1603–55* (Oxford, 1982) is the most valuable book on Cromwell's attitude to Jews.

The works that throw some light on Cromwell's last 'dark' years are C.H. Firth, 'Cromwell and the crown', *English Historical Review*, **17**, **18**, 1902, 1903; D. Underdown, 'Cromwell and the officers, February 1658', *English Historical Review*, **83**, 1968; A. Woolrych, 'Historical introduction' in *The Complete Prose Works of John Milton*, **7**, 1659–60 (Yale, 1980); 'Last quests for settlement 1657–60' in Aylmer, (ed.), *Interregnum* (see above); and R. Hutton, *The Restoration* (Oxford, 1985).

The impact of the Cromwellian regime on provincial England, Ireland and Scotland has received a great deal of attention. There are good studies of some English localities in the mid-seventeenth century, such as A. Everitt, *The Community of Kent and the Great Rebellion* (Leicester, 1966); D. Underdown, *Somerset during the Civil War and Interregnum* (David and Charles, Newton Abbot, 1973); J.S. Morrill, *Cheshire 1630–60* (Oxford, 1974); A. Fletcher, *A County Community at Peace and War: Sussex 1600–60* (Longman 1975); A. Hughes, *Politics, Society and Civil War in Warwickshire 1620–60* (Cambridge,1987); A. Coleby, *Central Government and the Localities: Hampshire 1649–89* (Cambridge, 1987); S. Roberts, *Recovery and Restoration in an English County: Devon*

Local Administration 1646–70 (Exeter, 1986). Some of these, though, are stronger on the period before 1650 than on the Protectorate. H.M. Reece, 'The military presence in England 1649–60', unpublished Oxford PhD thesis, 1981, and articles on the major-generals by D.W. Rannie in *English Historical Review*, **10**, 895; I. Roots in R.H. Parry (ed.), *After the English Civil War* (Macmillan, 1970) and A. Fletcher in D. Baker (ed.), *Religious Motivation (Studies in Church History*, **15**, 1978) are very useful. But much still remains to be done on the history of the localities in Cromwellian England. A. Fletcher, 'Oliver Cromwell and the localities' in Jones, Newitt and Roberts, (eds.), *Politics and People* (above) points the way for detailed work on the 1650s.

On Ireland and Scotland the best starting points are D. Stevenson, 'Cromwell, Scotland and Ireland' in Morrill (ed.), *Cromwell* (see above), who also supplies a full guide to further reading, and I.Roots, 'Union and disunion in the British Isles, 1637–60' in I. Roots (ed.), *'Into another mould': Aspects of the Interregnum* (Exeter, 1981). On Ireland I have found P.J. Corish's articles in T.W. Moody, F.X. Martin and F.J. Byrne (eds), *A New History of Ireland, 3, Early Modern Ireland 1534–1691* (Oxford, 1976) particularly helpful, together with T.C. Barnard, *Cromwellian Ireland, 1649–60,* (Oxford, 1975) and the relevant chapter in R. Foster, *Modern Ireland 1600–1972* (Penguin, 1988). F.D. Dow, *Cromwellian Scotland 1651–60* (John Donald, Edinburgh, 1979) has a good claim to be the standard work on its subject.

Cromwell's aims abroad have been the subject of protracted debate as has been seen. Easily the best, balanced survey is R. Crabtree, 'The idea of a Protestant foreign policy' in Roots (ed.), *Cromwell* (see above). This should be read together with M. Roberts, 'Cromwell and the Baltic', *English Historical Review*, **76**, 1961 and M. Roberts (ed.), *Swedish Diplomats at Cromwell's Court* (Royal Historical Society, Camden Society, 4th series, **36**, 1988). The limitations of C.P. Korr's book are indicated by its sub-title: *Cromwell and the New Model Foreign Policy: England's Policy Towards France 1649–58* (California, 1975). The best writing on the Western Design is K.O. Kupperman, 'Errand to the Indies: Puritan colonisation from Providence Island through the Western Design', *William and Mary Quarterly*, 3rd series, **45**, 1988.

Lastly, the most exciting – if exasperating – way of all of studying Cromwell is through the writings of his contemporaries and himself. There are accessible editions of the memoirs of Richard Baxter, the earl of Clarendon, Colonel John Hutchinson, Edmund Ludlow and Bulstrode Whitelocke. The most recent edition of twenty-six of Cromwell's speeches is by I. Roots, *Speeches of Oliver Cromwell* (Dent, 1989). There are three major editions of Cromwell's collected writings and speeches: C.L. Stainer (ed.), *Speeches of Oliver Cromwell 1644–58* (Oxford, 1901); *The Letters and Speeches of Oliver Cromwell with Elucidations by Thomas Carlyle Edited in Three Volumes . . . by S.C. Lomas* (3 vols, London, 1904); and W.C. Abbott (ed.), *The Writings and Speeches of Oliver Cromwell* (4 vols, Harvard, 1937–47; Oxford University Press reprint ed, 1989). On the merits of each, see J. Morrill, 'Textualizing and contextualizing Cromwell', *Historical Journal,* **33**, 1990.

INDEX